Cambridge Elements ≡

Elements in Defence Economics
edited by
Keith Hartley
University of York

HOW IMPORTANT ARE SUPERIOR NUMBERS?

A Reappraisal of Lanchester's Square Law

David L. I. Kirkpatrick
University College London

CAMBRIDGE
UNIVERSITY PRESS

CAMBRIDGE
UNIVERSITY PRESS

University Printing House, Cambridge CB2 8BS, United Kingdom

One Liberty Plaza, 20th Floor, New York, NY 10006, USA

477 Williamstown Road, Port Melbourne, VIC 3207, Australia

314–321, 3rd Floor, Plot 3, Splendor Forum, Jasola District Centre,
New Delhi – 110025, India

79 Anson Road, #06–04/06, Singapore 079906

Cambridge University Press is part of the University of Cambridge.

It furthers the University's mission by disseminating knowledge in the pursuit of
education, learning, and research at the highest international levels of excellence.

www.cambridge.org
Information on this title: www.cambridge.org/9781108977876
DOI: 10.1017/9781108973458

© David L. I. Kirkpatrick 2021

First published 2021

A catalogue record for this publication is available from the British Library.

ISBN 978-1-108-97787-6 Paperback
ISSN 2632-332X (online)
ISSN 2632-3311 (print)

How Important are Superior Numbers?

A Reappraisal of Lanchester's Square Law

Elements in Defence Economics

DOI: 10.1017/9781108973458
First published online: February 2021

David L. I. Kirkpatrick
University College London
Author for correspondence: David L. I. Kirkpatrick, kpbroadoak@gmail.com

Abstract: A century ago, Frederick Lanchester formulated a mathematical model of combat which suggested that the combat power of a military force was proportional to the product of the individual effectiveness of the units in the force and the square of the number of units deployed. This model reinforced a long-established faith in the importance of superior numbers. However, successive historical studies failed to identify any clear relationship between the numbers and losses in opposing forces. This Element analyses American Civil War battles, and shows that the ratio of losses incurred was inversely proportional to the ratio of numbers effectively engaged. This result demonstrates that the numbers of fighting units in a military force are less important than the ability of those units to get into action and inflict losses on the enemy. This result demonstrates the limitations of the Square Law, and should prevent it from being applied indiscriminately.

Keywords: American Civil War, superior numbers, Lanchester's Square Law, quality versus quantity, defence policy

ISBNs: 9781108977876 (PB), 9781108973458 (OC)
ISSNs: 2632-332X (online), 2632-3311 (print)

Contents

Contents

1 Introduction

Throughout history, each nation has organised its armed forces to achieve the optimal balance between the number of fighting men deployed and the quality of these men and their equipment. Long ago, the balance was often constrained by a shortage of resources (such as horses or mineral ores) or by the limitations of the available technology. In recent decades, it has become more difficult to identify the optimal balance because the ever-increasing unit cost of top-quality weapon systems constrains the number which can be procured within a national government's limited budget. The difficulty may become even greater in future years with the advent of mobile and autonomous weapon systems, which might vary widely in size, unit cost and combat capability, and which might augment or replace some components of current military forces.

It is important for any nation to strike the right balance between quality and quantity. Armed forces which are numerous but poorly armed are generally doomed to bloody defeat, whereas small and expensively equipped forces are vulnerable to accidents, unserviceability and diseconomies of scale. Today, any nation must strike a balance between the quantity of its fighting units (such as battalions, warships or combat aircraft) and the quality of those units (which is a synthesis of the performance of their equipment, the skills of their personnel and the leadership of their commanders). The optimal balance depends on the nature of the threat(s) to the nation's security and to its vital interests, on the assistance which it can expect from allies, on the potential scenarios of symmetrical and asymmetrical warfare, and on the scale of the resources which the nation chooses to allocate to its defence budget. In practice, the chosen balance may be affected by the nation's historical experience and traditions, by institutional inertia, and by pressure from political, military and industrial factions with particular ideologies or interests.

Early in the twentieth century, Lanchester formulated a pair of mathematical models of combat which were intended to help contemporary military planners to achieve the optimal balance between quality and quantity in their national armed forces (Lanchester 1916). The particular model which appeared relevant to contemporary battles between firing lines of infantry and artillery, and between columns of ironclad warships, was the Square Law model. This model suggested that the combat power of a military force was proportional to the product of the individual effectiveness of the fighting units in the force and the square of the number of fighting units deployed. In the decades which followed, the Square Law model was frequently cited by politicians (such as Stalin, who claimed that 'quantity has a quality of its own') to stress the importance of superior numbers, but such politicians generally failed to appreciate the limitations of the Square Law model in representing real battles.

Despite the failures of multiple subsequent studies (discussed in Section 5) which attempted to demonstrate the validity of Lanchester's Square Law model, it continued through the twentieth century to influence the analysis of military operations and to confuse debates on defence equipment procurement, often fuelling arguments that the latest equipment designs were too expensive and that the military staffs should constrain their requirements. As national governments in the twenty-first century continue to struggle to accommodate the high unit cost of procuring military equipment (£100 M for a combat aircraft and £3,000 M for a Royal Navy aircraft carrier, without its aircraft) within limited defence budgets, it is appropriate to reconsider the validity of Lanchester's Square Law model and to illuminate its limitations.

This Element outlines in Section 2 how conditions of combat have developed over past centuries, and how these developments have changed the relative importance of the quality and quantity of fighting units deployed. It discusses how, in some particular historical scenarios, victory was determined principally by the relative effectiveness (quality) of the opposing fighting units, but in other scenarios victory was determined principally by massed firepower and hence by the numbers (quantity) in the opposing forces. Section 3 describes Lanchester's two combat models which represent these two alternative scenarios – the Square Law model representing aimed fire between opposing arrays of fighting units, and the Linear Law model representing either a succession of duels between opposing fighting units or the random bombardment of opposing deployed forces – and Section 4 discusses the inherent problems of validating either of these combat models. Section 5 reviews earlier attempts to compare the predictions of Lanchester's models with the results of historical battles and campaigns, and notes their failure to identify any clear relationship, as predicted by the Square Law model, between the ratio of the strengths of the opposing forces and the ratio of the casualties which they sustained.

Section 6 identifies the reasons why the American Civil War (ACW) in 1861–5 is the most suitable focus for the more-rigorous analysis presented in this Element, and Section 7 describes the methodology of that analysis and its result. This new analysis demonstrates for the first time that, in open-field battles of the American Civil War, the Union/Confederate loss ratio declined as the Union/ Confederate ratio of troops engaged increased, roughly in accordance with Lanchester's Square Law. Sections 8 and 9 present the results of similar analyses of some other wars in the eighteenth and nineteenth centuries. Because these wars had fewer battles, and some of the loss ratios were distorted by particular circumstances, these supporting analyses do not provide conclusive support for Lanchester's Square Law but they are consistent with it. Section 10 discusses how the Square Law may have influenced military decision-making in the twentieth century. Section 11 reviews the results of the analyses in Sections 7, 8 and 9 and of the associated implications. Finally Section 12 presents the principal conclusions, and emphasises the importance of recognising that Lanchester's Square Law is valid only for some particular conditions of combat, and should not be applied indiscriminately in national defence planning and policy.

2 Historical Background to the Quality/Quantity Quandary

2.1 Warfare in the Classical and Medieval Periods

In these periods, armies could include contingents of heavy infantry and cavalry, both of which were armoured and equipped for hand-to-hand combat, and contingents of light infantry and cavalry relying principally on missile weapons (bows, slings and javelins). Some armies were formed almost entirely of one of these types; others included up to four types in proportions depending on the current availability of equipment (for example, heavy cavalry became more important after the introduction of the stirrup). Throughout these periods, missile weapons could inflict some losses and annoyance (and occasionally could defeat forces with fragile morale) but in general victory in land battles was achieved primarily by hand-to-hand combat between masses of heavy infantry or cavalry. In such combat, the decisive factor was the relative effectiveness of the soldiers in the front ranks, who engaged their opponents in a sequence of individual duels. The effectiveness of an individual infantryman (which was a synthesis of his bravery, skill and equipment) was much more important than the numbers in the opposing armies because only the infantry in the front ranks were actively engaged. It followed that soldiers who were better-armed and better-trained (such as Spartan hoplites or Roman legionaries) could generally defeat any number of enemies with lesser capabilities. Higher-quality forces were occasionally defeated if they were disadvantaged by surprise, unfavourable terrain or inept leadership, and these defeats often feature prominently in reviews of military history precisely because they were unusual and remarkable.

In the medieval period, and occasionally earlier, victory was often achieved by the shock action of heavy cavalry charging into close combat with enemy cavalry or with disordered infantry. In such close combat, victory depended on the fighting abilities of the individual cavalryman, and also on the speed and power of his horse. The skill and bravery of individual heroes fighting mounted or on foot (and even the lethality of their weapons) was extolled in Greek epics, Viking sagas and Arthurian legends. It was axiomatic that their individual fighting qualities were of paramount importance.

In the classical and medieval periods, naval warfare in the Mediterranean was dominated by the oared galley. Victory in sea battles was generally determined by the speed and manoeuvrability of the individual galleys which sought to ram and sink their opponents (or to disable them by smashing their oars). The Romans devised methods of trapping enemy ships (using a corvus or harpex) to enable the decisive actions to be fought by boarding parties, fighting in the same hand-to-hand manner as in land battles, and such actions were decided by the fighting abilities of individual marines. Galleys deployed by rival states increased in size (from biremes to triremes to quinqueremes) as the advantages of increasing the fighting strength of individual galleys became apparent, and they benefitted from successive improvements to the crews' weaponry (notably composite bows and Byzantine flamethrowers).

Off the coasts of Northern Europe, the stormy seas generally precluded the operation of oared galleys using rams. Viking chiefs and their rivals fought sea battles only in relatively calm and sheltered waters – in such battles each longship grappled an enemy ship so that warriors could board and fight hand-to-hand on the enemy's deck. It was advantageous to have larger and higher-sided longships which offered some protection from enemy missiles and which made it more difficult for enemies to board. Larger ships often won even when outnumbered.

In northern seas, medieval kings used large sailing warships as floating troop carriers to bring their soldiers into close action against enemy ships, using missiles to deplete the enemy crews before capturing their ships by boarding. Such actions essentially replicated land battles in a maritime environment, and victory was primarily determined, as in Viking battles, by the fighting abilities of individual soldiers

2.2 Warfare in the Gunpowder Age

The introduction of muskets and cannon using gunpowder transformed warfare; thereafter battles on land and sea were decided primarily by firepower. Through the eighteenth century and part of the nineteenth, land warfare was dominated by infantry armed with smoothbore muskets and bayonets, supported by cavalry with swords and lances and by smoothbore artillery firing solid shot, shells and canister. Victory in land battles was determined primarily by the firepower of the infantry and artillery, though cavalry sometimes had the opportunity to make decisive charges. The numbers in the opposing armies became more important because the ranges of muskets and cannons enabled larger numbers of soldiers to employ converging fire against fewer enemies. In the period 1700–1850, when the armed forces of all European nations were armed with similar weaponry, it was realised that the larger force was likely to be victorious, though it was appreciated that other factors (training, morale, leadership, etc.)

were also important. Voltaire could conclude that 'God was on the side of the big battalions' (Voltaire 1770) and Napoleon always sought to concentrate superior numbers at the decisive point in a campaign (Chandler 2002). The importance of superior numbers was emphasised by the victories achieved by the American and French revolutionary armies in which large numbers of soldiers (albeit imperfectly trained and disciplined) had weapons similar to those of their potential oppressors, whereas earlier revolts by exploited peasants had consistently failed. In this period, victory was determined largely by the relative size of the opposing armies and by the relative skill of the generals in motivating and manoeuvring their forces effectively. Generals, such as Frederick the Great and Napoleon, who won against superior numbers received special honour and glory.

In the wars between European nations in the early gunpowder age, it was expected that a battle would generally be won by the larger army deployed on the battlefield. However in wars against underdeveloped nations with inferior weapons the Europeans were generally victorious against the odds. In this period, Spanish forces were able to exploit the superior quality of their weaponry to conquer much of Central and South America, defeating native forces which had vastly superior numbers but were poorly armed. Concurrently, other European nations forcibly established colonies and trading posts on the coasts of Africa, Asia and North America. Later the quality of European armies enabled them to win victories in India, North Africa and elsewhere against much-larger native forces, some of whom had the same weapons as the Europeans but who had not yet fully adopted European methods of organisation, discipline and command structures (James 1998, pp. 142–3).

Sea warfare in this period was dominated by large sailing warships carrying large numbers of heavy guns and planning to sink or disable enemy ships by gunfire; severely damaged ships tended to surrender and could then be boarded without resistance. In firefights between such warships, the decisive factors were the size of their guns, the rate and accuracy of fire, and the robustness of the ships themselves, relative to their opponents. The limited arcs of fire of naval guns on these warships meant that they could fire their broadsides only at one enemy warship, and superior numbers could only be effective if a skilful admiral (like Rodney or Nelson) was able to institute a melee involving his whole fleet against fewer enemy ships. In this period, the fighting abilities of a nation's individual warships and their crews were more important than the relative size of the opposing fleets, and British admirals were almost always prepared to accept battle against superior numbers (Admiral Sir John Jervis faced adverse odds of 15:27 at Cape St. Vincent in 1797).

2.3 Warfare in the Modern Age

From the middle of the nineteenth century, a series of technical developments (rifled muskets with Minie bullets, breech-loading and repeater mechanisms, and smokeless powder) enabled rifles to fire faster and further, and concurrent developments vastly increased the range, accuracy and rate of fire of artillery. After the introduction of rifled muskets, cavalry rarely charged infantry on the battlefield; such charges were always costly and were almost invariably unsuccessful. In the World Wars of the twentieth century, cavalry achieved no significant battlefield successes, except against infantry who were demoralised, disorganised or poorly armed. Artillery became increasingly dominant and Victorian military histories recognised the enhanced power of artillery by normally citing the number of guns with an army as well as the number of soldiers. In this period of rapid development, armies with obsolete equipment were heavily defeated (like the Russians in 1853, and the Austrians in 1866). By the end of the nineteenth century, it was arguable that future battlefields would be dominated by artillery and machine guns; the 1884 Maxim machine gun was considered to be equivalent in firepower to twenty-four riflemen and the 1912 Vickers to forty riflemen, respectively (Mead 2008, p. 160), though conservative soldiers believed that bayonets and sabres would remain important. In the decades prior to World War I, many politicians had an exaggerated respect for the size of the Imperial Russian army, and expected that the 'Russian steamroller' would be able to crush any enemy through sheer weight of numbers. Better-informed generals appreciated that current weapon developments demanded decisions on whether they should use any additional resources to increase the size of their armies or to give them better equipment; those generals knew (even if most contemporary politicians and journalists did not) that assessing the combat power of an army was not simply a matter of counting the army's personnel, and that any such assessment must take account of the quality of the soldiers' weapon systems, training and leadership.

In the latter part of the nineteenth century, there were several major wars between developed nations which were all able to equip their forces with the latest weaponry, and there were also many 'little wars' between imperialist forces equipped with advanced weapon systems (such as machine guns, rifled artillery and ironclad warships) and the indigenous forces of less-developed nations which did not have similar weaponry. In such (asymmetric) wars, the better-armed imperialist forces were almost invariably victorious, despite the superior numbers and the undisputed bravery of their various native enemies. In these wars there was generally a huge difference in the quality of the weapons used by the opposing forces, and consequently the poorly armed forces often suffered horrendous losses. The Battle of the Little Big Horn in 1876 was an exception because the 7th US Cavalry had single-shot carbines whereas some of their Native American opponents had repeating rifles; the 7th US Cavalry was outgunned as well as outnumbered.

At sea, successive generations of warships in the late nineteenth and early twentieth centuries had ever-larger guns and ever-thicker armour, and out-classed fleets were easy targets for their more-modern enemies. In August 1914, a British fleet of four armoured cruisers declined to engage a single German battle cruiser which had bigger guns and thicker armour. At his court martial, the British admiral's decision was considered to be justifiable (and that ruling was retrospectively endorsed by the relative fragility at Jutland of British armoured cruisers and German battle cruisers). In November 1914, a pair of British armoured cruisers was destroyed near Coronel by an opposing pair of German armoured cruisers which had been built five years later and were correspondingly much more powerful. A month later, near the Falkland Islands, the same pair of German armoured cruisers was sunk by two British battle cruisers with 305 mm (12 inch) guns to overwhelm the German 210 mm (8.2 inch). In both these battles, the victors suffered only a few sailors killed or wounded, while almost all of the defeated sailors were killed or drowned (Bennett 1967, pp. 39 and 156). Before the potentially decisive battle of Jutland in June 1916, the admiral commanding the German High Seas Fleet only reluctantly allowed a squadron of six obsolete pre-dreadnought battleships to join the twenty-one dreadnought battleships and battlecruisers in his line of battle (to face thirty-seven British dreadnoughts); the admiral regarded the pre-dreadnoughts as essentially useless, and they were left behind when the High Seas Fleet subsequently sortied in August (Halpern 1994, pp. 315 and 330). In this period, it was expected that in naval battles between warships with similar fighting ability the larger fleet would generally be victorious, but that warships with bigger guns and thicker armour could defeat any number of inferior opponents (initially demonstrated by the ironclads 'Nemesis' in 1840 and 'Virginia' in 1862). Only the French were (briefly) convinced that a large fleet of fast torpedo boats could defeat British battleships by sheer weight of numbers.

In the twentieth century, the development of military equipment accelerated, and land warfare (except in urban areas) was increasingly dominated by the long-range firepower of artillery, armoured fighting vehicles (AFV) and anti-tank (AT) guns. Units whose firepower was outclassed were generally heavily defeated. But even on the fire-swept battlefields of the twentieth century, tactical victories were often achieved by the courage and capabilities of front-line infantrymen, such as Leutnant Rommel and Sergeant York. In World War II, the exceptional skills of individual AFV commanders and the performance of their vehicles allowed these commanders to achieve high totals of enemy AFV destroyed, indicating that in combats between opposing AFV the quality of the crews and their vehicles remained important. Obersturmfuhrer Michael Wittman, for example, destroyed 138 enemy tanks (Ford 1998, p. 78) before he was himself killed.

In the same period, advances in mechanical, electrical and electronic engineering created several new specialist classes of fighting unit and increased the tempo of land/air warfare. In land battles, victory increasingly depended on the ability of a commander to achieve cooperative synergy between the diverse weapon and sensor systems at his disposal. In former times, land warfare might have been compared to a stately minuet; today it more resembles a fast-paced three-dimensional Scottish eightsome reel, involving multiple interactions between many different classes of fighting unit. Similarly, at sea, admirals now have to coordinate the operation of multiple classes of fighting unit above, on and below the surface of the sea. During the twentieth century, dramatic developments in electronic sensors and communications systems have allowed modern commanders to direct their military forces more effectively. Following the 'Revolution in Military Affairs' at the end of the twentieth century, all classes of fighting unit have been digitally linked to facilitate information exchange and effective coordination of Allied forces in rapidly changing situations during symmetric and asymmetric operations in the Middle East.

As air warfare developed through the twentieth century, victory in the aerial dogfights of World War I depended principally on the skill of individual pilots and on the performance of their aircraft and guns. Hence particularly talented pilots, designated as 'aces', could survive multiple aerial duels, and accumulate an impressive total of kills. For example, Major Edward Mannock scored seventy-three kills and Baron Manfred von Richthofen scored eighty before they were both killed (Gilbert 1994). Some of the air combats in World War II were more structured, with large formations of bombers defending themselves with thousands of machine guns; in such combats the relative number of bombers and attacking fighters was probably significant. Numbers would also be important if modern air combats involved opposing fleets of aircraft exchanging salvos of long-range missiles, but in practice such combats have tended to involve individual opposing aircraft (or small formations) where the quality of the aircrew and their aircraft is paramount. Superior quality of aircraft, weapons and aircrew yielded very favourable kill ratios in 1982 for British aircraft over the Falkland Islands and for Israeli aircraft over the Bekaa Valley in the same year.

2.4 Synopsis

This review of military history suggests that during some periods in some environments victory was primarily decided by the fighting abilities (or quality) of individual fighting units (infantrymen, cavalrymen, ships or aircraft). In other scenarios dominated by firepower, victory was determined largely by the numbers (or quantity) of the fighting units with similar weaponry deployed by the opposing forces. However, even in battles dominated by firepower, victory could be determined by the opposing forces' leadership, tactics and other factors.

In the century before Lanchester formulated his combat models, it was firepower which decided the outcomes of land battles between firing lines of infantry and artillery and which decided the outcomes of sea battles between lines of battleships. When Lanchester proposed his models, the potential of aircraft, submarines and 'land ironclads' could only be conjectured and the advent of guided missiles and spy satellites was entirely unforeseen. In the relatively simple military scenarios familiar to Lanchester and to contemporary politicians, it seemed plausible that the Square Law model was sufficiently representative to guide the development of cost-effective military forces.

Today, the three-dimensional military environment is much more complicated and major operations (such as the 1944 invasion of Normandy) involve land, sea and air forces working in close cooperation; their success can depend on fortifications, logistics and disinformation as well as on the quantity and quality of the fighting units. In this very complex environment, the debate on the relative importance of the quality and the quantity of defence forces continues unabated. The military, naval and air staffs tend to demand the best available equipment to give their fellow servicemen the advantage in any future war. Politicians tend to favour impressively numerous forces, intended to enhance national prestige. Some journalists claim that current equipment is expensively 'baroque' (Kaldor 1982), having been extravagantly designed to meet over-ambitious requirements, and they deplore the ever-decreasing scale of the land, sea and air forces which smaller nations like the United Kingdom can afford. Naval staffs appreciate that a small fleet relying on a few major fighting units is vulnerable to accident, unserviceability and surprise, and that a battle at sea can be won or lost by a single crucial decision or a single lucky hit; thus reliance on small naval forces is an inherently risky strategy. Conversely, military staffs have always understood that large armies, if they are assigned to fight in an underdeveloped area far from their own bases, can be difficult to deploy, to supply during operations and to repatriate afterwards. All officers and analysts understand that a marginal superiority in the quality of a task force's equipment (in firepower, mobility, sensors or communications) could give that force an important, perhaps a decisive, advantage in symmetric or asymmetric warfare. However they appreciate that an additional 10 per cent added to a weapon system's performance typically generates an additional 33 per cent in its unit cost (Augustine 1983, p. 47), so achieving that marginal superiority might be an unacceptable burden on a limited defence budget.

In the interdependent political, military and financial dilemmas characteristic of national defence reviews, confused decision makers may be influenced by the simplistic appeal of Lanchester's Square Law (just as in the country of the blind, the one-eyed man is king). It is therefore important for this analysis to propagate a better understanding of the Square Law and its limitations.

3 Lanchester's Combat Models

3.1 Lanchester's Achievements

Frederick William Lanchester (1868–1946) was born in Lewisham, London. He became a distinguished engineer, and was chosen to be a Fellow of the Royal Society. He developed the first successful motor car in Britain in 1895, and founded a motor car company which produced 400 Lanchester cars in the early years of the twentieth century. He then turned his attention to aeronautics and wrote a two-volume book, *Aerial Flight* (published in 1907 and 1908), which presented the basic concepts of boundary layers, induced drag and flight dynamics, and thus laid the foundations of aircraft design. After these scientific achievements, he studied warfare, and his book *Aircraft in Warfare* included mathematical models of different types of combat (Lanchester 1916). He hoped that these combat models would assist British military and naval staffs in planning the future of the national armed forces.

3.2 Lanchester's Square Law

Lanchester's mathematical model of modern warfare proposed that the rate at which battle losses were sustained by one force was equal to the product of the number of fighting units in the opposing force and the individual effectiveness of those units. He expected that this model would be valid for contemporary scenarios in the early twentieth century, such as battles between firing lines of infantry from opposing armies or between parallel lines of battleships from opposing navies. It might also be valid for World War II battles between opposing fleets of armoured fighting vehicles (AFV) in the deserts of North Africa or on the steppes of the Ukraine. This model implicitly assumed that all of the fighting units present were deployed within range of an enemy unit, and were thus able to engage the enemy. If at any stage of the battle the numbers of

Blue and Red units are represented by the parameters B and R, Lanchester's Square Law model suggests that:

Rate of casualties to Blue force = Number of Red units x Effectiveness of Red units.

Hence, $dB/dt = -Rr$ and $dR/dt = -Bb$, $dB/dR = r/b \, (R/B)$.   (1)

The parameter r, representing the individual effectiveness of Red units, incorporates the performance of their weaponry, their combat skill and motivation, their tactical doctrine, the competence of their commanders, and the vulnerability of the Blue units. It follows that the parameter r would be smaller if the Blue units occupied a fortified position. From this model, Lanchester concluded (by integrating the above equation, and neglecting second-order terms), that:

Blue losses = $(r\mathbf{R}/b\mathbf{B})$ Red losses   (2)

and

Blue attrition = $(r\mathbf{R}^2/b\mathbf{B}^2)$ Red attrition.   (3)

In equations (2) and (3), the parameters $\mathbf{B}$ and $\mathbf{R}$ are the initial numbers of Blue and Red units in the opposing Blue and Red forces. Other factors (such as morale, supply, terrain etc.) being equal, the force which sustained the higher level of attrition would normally be defeated; armies in battle only occasionally achieved their objectives despite suffering higher attrition (thus winning a 'Pyrrhic' victory). Hence the Blue force was more likely to be victorious if the attrition of the Red force was higher, and if

$b\mathbf{B}^2 > r\mathbf{R}^2$.

However, even when the Blue force is apparently stronger according to this equation, it might still be defeated if the Red commander made a particularly effective manoeuvre or if the Blue force was consistently unlucky.

It follows from the Square Law that the strength of a military force can be assessed as equal to the product of the individual effectiveness of its fighting units and the **square** of the number of units in the force. This Square Law reinforced the faith of contemporary generals in the importance of superior numbers, and in the well-established principle that they should assemble the largest possible force before any important battle. Lanchester considered that his 'Square Law' model applied to modern battles between opposing military or naval forces relying principally on aimed firepower, but it implicitly assumed that the rival commanders involved had succeeded in bringing all of their forces into action together (or had the same proportion of their respective forces in action). Throughout history, generals and admirals have struggled to achieve the goal of bringing all of their fighting units into action together, but in practice it was never a straightforward process; the number of units actually engaged was often considerably less than the number available. In the twentieth century, improvements in electronic surveillance and communications have enabled land, sea and air forces to be directed more effectively, but not all of the practical difficulties have been overcome.

Between the World Wars, Lanchester's mathematical conclusion on the importance of numbers was welcomed by those politicians and generals who were suspicious of new-fangled weaponry and who sought status from the sheer scale of their armed forces (as Mussolini in 1936 boasted of his eight million bayonets). Admirals were less impressed. They had realised in the middle of the nineteenth century that one ironclad could demolish any number of wooden ships of the line. They were aware that in World War I, modern warships had easily defeated older ones (see Section 2.2) and they accepted that in sea battles quality (in terms of the warships' speed, armour and gun power, as well as the motivation and training of their crews) was extremely important.

3.3 Lanchester's Linear Law

Lanchester also proposed an alternative mathematical model to represent battles involving the random bombardment of opposing forces. In this model, the rate of loss to the Blue force is related to the number and effectiveness of the Red units and to the density of deployment of Blue units in the target area, and vice versa.

Hence $dB/dt = -RrB$ and $dR/dt = -BbR$,

$$dB/dR = r/b \tag{4}$$

$$\text{Blue losses} = (r/b) \text{ Red losses} \tag{5}$$

In such battles, the combat strength of a force is equal to the product of the individual effectiveness of each unit and the number of units in the force, and the Blue force is likely to be victorious if $b\mathbf{B} > r\mathbf{R}$.

In battles which could be represented by this Linear Law, the relative number of units in the opposing forces is accordingly less important.

This Linear Law model also represents the outcome of a battle consisting of a succession of duels, which was perhaps characteristic of hand-to-hand combat in the classical and medieval periods or of air combat between gun-armed fighter aircraft in the twentieth century wars. In these types of battles involving successive duels, particularly expert heroes or aces (such as

Achilles or Baron von Richthofen) could account for large numbers of their opponents.

3.4 Validation

In principle, either of Lanchester's Laws could be validated by comparing its prediction with the results of a series of battles for which the initial strengths and the final losses of the forces involved are known with reasonable accuracy. The Square Law, for example, predicts that

Blue losses = $(r\mathbf{R}/b\mathbf{B})$ Red losses. (6)

It is convenient to plot the losses and initial numbers in battles between Blue and Red forces on logarithmic scales to determine if the relationship is linear in accordance with equation (7):

Log (Blue/Red loss ratio) = Log (r/b) – Log (**Blue/Red** initial strength ratio). (7)

Hence, if the Square Law were valid, the data from a series of battles between the same opposing armies (such that the Blue/Red ratio of individual effectiveness was virtually constant) would show the Blue/Red loss ratio decreasing linearly on a logarithmic scale as the **Blue/Red** initial strength ratio increases.

3.5 Calculation of the Ratio of Individual Effectiveness

From equations (2) and (5), linking the Blue/Red ratio of losses to the **Blue/Red** ratio of the initial strengths of the opposing forces, the ratio r/b of the individual effectiveness of Red and Blue forces is:
    for the Square Law model:

Log (r/b) = log (Blue/Red loss ratio) + log (**Blue/Red** initial strength ratio), (8)

and for the Linear Law model:

Log (r/b) = log (Blue/Red losses). (9)

The effectiveness ratio does not reflect the personal bravery of the Blue and Red soldiers, nor the justice of their respective causes, but is determined by a host of factors, including the soldiers' equipment, training, tactical doctrine and the expertise of their commanders.

3.6 Applications of Lanchester's Combat Models

The international situation in the late 1930s demanded urgent analysis of the desirable characteristics of new weapon systems, and this encouraged the development in the UK and elsewhere of several variants of

Lanchester's combat models. These variants attempted to represent more accurately the engagement scenarios typical of land, sea and air warfare. During the Cold War, the rival superpowers used computer models of theatre-level campaigns to assess the balance of their conventional (non-nuclear) military forces, and hence to guide their allocation of resources across the range of available weapon systems. Such models had to keep their complexity and running times within acceptable limits, so they generally used some relatively simple Lanchester models to resolve the outcomes of low-level engagements. This reliance on Lanchester models to influence large defence budgets stimulated a torrent of nearly 200 published papers within three decades (Haysman 1980). However, throughout this period, the prevalent uncritical faith in the popular Square Law model was not supported by any demonstration of its validity, because of the problems discussed in Section 4.

4 Problems in Validation

Validation of Lanchester's Laws for land warfare would ideally require data on a series of battles between the armies of the same two combatant nations (so that the quality of the opposing troops, the effectiveness of their equipment and the other factors which determine the combat effectiveness of an army, aside from its numerical strength, were essentially constant). For a conclusive validation, this series of battles should include a wide range of strength ratios, but in general an army which was heavily outnumbered often chose to retreat rather than to fight at a disadvantage. Hence the strength ratios in historical battles are generally not far from unity (except in those asymmetric battles between well-armed and poorly armed forces where the latter hoped to prevail by superior numbers).

It has proved difficult to validate either of Lanchester's Laws because for battles in the classical and medieval periods there are generally no reliable data on the strength and losses of the opposing forces, and because in modern battles the forces involved are so heterogeneous (deploying several classes of weapon systems) that modelling involves excessive complexity and a multitude of assumptions. In the eighteenth and nineteenth centuries however, there are credible (albeit imperfect) data on the strengths and losses of the combatant armies, and those armies typically included only three combat arms (infantry, cavalry and artillery) which were generally deployed in similar proportions. In this period, a single total is reasonably representative of an army's strength.

Unfortunately for modern analysts (though mercifully for the soldiers involved) many of the wars in the eighteenth and nineteenth centuries were non-ideological and were fought for limited objectives; hence they were often decided by only a few major battles, supplemented by sieges and manoeuvres. The ratio of the losses incurred by the armies in any particular battle may be affected by special circumstances such as fortification, surprise, terrain or a particularly incompetent commander. All of these factors tend to obscure the effect of the relative strength of the opposing armies. Short wars with few battles do not provide an adequate database for analysis.

Even when one of the eighteenth and nineteenth century wars has sufficient battles to form an adequate database, there are often difficulties with the historical records of the strengths and losses of the opposing armies. From the eighteenth century onward, the historical records of a battle generally esti- mate the total strength of each of the opposing armies from a recent muster roll, with an (approximate) allowance for subsequent sickness and straggling. The quoted total strength of an army may include irregular units (like the Russian Cossacks) which were present with the army but were not expected to do more than skirmishing. The data on the number of troops present may be misleading because some contingents were not brought into action at all, or were in action for only part of the battle; this problem particularly affects battles which lasted for a long time during which reinforcements for one army or the other arrived at intervals. It is sometimes possible to estimate how the ratio of the numbers of soldiers engaged varied through the course of a battle, and hence to derive a representative time-averaged ratio. Generally analysts must assume that the ratio of the total numbers which were engaged by the end of the battle is the best available measure of the relative strengths of the opposing armies.

Historical records of the armies' losses in battle may be inaccurate, incom- plete or distorted by the wishful thinking of generals. Such records estimate the total losses of each of the opposing armies, but they often also estimate separate totals for killed, wounded and missing. The latter category generally does not distinguish between soldiers who were killed unobserved by their comrades, soldiers who were captured (wounded or unwounded) during the battle as a direct result of the fighting and the others who were captured or who deserted from their units during a disorderly retreat resulting from a defeat. The numbers lost during a retreat depended principally on the morale of the defeated army and on the terrain which it had to cross (which might or might not favour a sustained pursuit), rather than on the firepower of the victorious army. In principle, unwounded prisoners captured during a battle and soldiers who went missing during a retreat should be excluded from the data used to validate Lanchester's combat models, because these losses did not arise directly from the enemy's firepower. In practice, the different categories of 'missing' cannot generally be distinguished (except in a few special cases where the losses in one category are particularly notable, and hence were specially recorded).

Validation of either of Lanchester's Laws for naval warfare is even more difficult. Even in those eighteenth and nineteenth century wars which featured several land battles between combatant nations, naval battles were even less numerous and were often significantly affected by the variable conditions of wind and weather. It has proved impossible to assemble an adequate database on the numbers and losses in naval battles in any of these wars.

5 Some Past Attempts at Validating Lanchester's Combat Models

There have been numerous attempts to explore whether Lanchester's models realistically predicted the losses inflicted on opposing armies in historical battles. Willard analysed the reported strengths and casualties in land battles fought between 1618 and 1905, mostly between European armies (Willard 1962). This array of results excluded sieges and attacks on fortified positions, but it included armies with diverse variations in weaponry, organisation and other factors which predictably obscured the effect of the strength ratio. The outcomes for Willard's 938 open-field battles showed only a weak relationship between the loss ratios and strength ratios in different battles, whereas the Lanchester Square Law model (considered appropriate to such gunpowder-age battles) predicted that the loss ratio should be inversely proportional to the strength ratio.

Several analysts have studied the outcomes of amphibious assaults by US forces on Japanese-garrisoned islands in the Pacific during World War II (Weiss 1957, Engel 1954 and Kishi 1961). The results, which must have been influenced by the robustness and sophistication of the Japanese fortifications and by the scale of US naval and air support for each of the different landings, were too scattered to provide a definitive validation beyond confirming that the US loss rate decreased as the Japanese defenders were progressively annihilated. But there is considerable doubt about the day-to-day variation in the strengths of the opposing forces, and it proved impossible to identify any credible relationship between the strength ratios and the ratios of daily losses.

Others have compared the results of sixty engagements in the 1943–4 Italian campaign (Fain 1977) and have analysed the course of the 1944–5 Ardennes campaign (Fricker 1998). Both tried to compare the German/Allied casualty ratio with the ratio of the 'combat power' of the forces engaged; the estimates of 'combat power' were derived from the heterogeneous composition of the opposing forces and involved multiple judgements of the relative effectiveness of riflemen, artillery, armoured fighting vehicles and aircraft. These two studies did not discover any robust relationship between casualty ratios and combat power ratios.

From estimates of the daily losses suffered by United States Marines and by North Korean forces over the twenty days following the Inchon landing, it was concluded (Busse 1971) that North Korean losses were unaffected by the (small) variations in the strength of the Marines at the beginning of each day due to their earlier losses and reinforcements. His conclusions, like those of the World War II studies cited previously, were weakened by unreliability of the data on enemy losses.

Two analysts (Weiss 1966 and Kirkpatrick 1985) compared the strength ratios and loss ratios in the major battles of the American Civil War (ACW); this war is particularly suitable for an assessment of the validity of the Square Law (as discussed in Section 6). Both relied on Livermore's (1901) classic study of the numbers and losses in the ACW. This study analyses 63 battles and campaigns in which 1,000 or more soldiers were hit on either side (thus excluding skirmishes which can be determined by a fortuitous manoeuvre or a particular topography). Both Weiss and Kirkpatrick perforce excluded battles for which data on strength or losses were missing, and both also excluded assaults on fortified lines in which the outcome was more likely to be determined by the strength of the fortifications than by the relative number of troops involved. Weiss considered twenty-seven 'meeting engagements' and found no clear relationship between the loss ratios and the numbers ratios of the opposing armies.

Kirkpatrick was more selective, and excluded some additional battles where there was credible evidence of field fortifications, some battles where there were relatively large proportions of missing (who might or might not have been killed or wounded) and two more which were affected by special circumstances (at Richmond, Kentucky, where the Union troops were untrained recruits but the Confederates were veterans; and at Cedar Creek, Virginia, where the Confederate army achieved a devastating surprise attack). These exclusions reduced his database to sixteen open-field battles, for which the results are shown in Table 1.

Figure 1 presents the Union/Confederate (U/C) loss ratios for these battles plotted against the corresponding Union/Confederate strength ratios and shows that the loss ratio varies only slightly with the strength ratio, rather than being inversely proportional to the strength ratio as predicted by Lanchester's Square Law in equation (7). This unexpected and unwelcome result partially undermined faith in the Square Law.

In 1985, Kirkpatrick rationalised this result by pointing out that in battles between unequal forces the commander of the larger force inevitably had greater difficulties in synchronising the assembly of his force on the battlefield,

Table 1 Livermore's data on numbers and losses in 16 open-field ACW battles

Date	Battle	Log U/C strength	Log U/C loss
10/08/61	Wilson's Creek	−0.33	−0.09
07/03/62	Pea Ridge	−0.09	0.290
06–07/04/62	Shiloh	0.18	0.02
04/05/62	Williamsburg	0.11	0.08
31/05–01/06/62	Fair Oaks	0	−0.12
09/08/62	Cedar Mountain	−0.32	0.12
14/09/62	South Mountain	0.18	−0.04
16/09/62	Antietam	0.16	0
08/10/62	Perryville	0.36	0.07
07/12/62	Prairie Grove	0	0
31/12/62	Stones River	0.08	0
01/05–04/05/63	Chancellorsville & Fredericksburg	0.23	0.02
01/07–03/07/63	Gettysburg	0.05	−0.11
19/09/63	Chickamauga	−0.06	−0.17
09/04/64	Pleasant Hill	−0.05	0
12/05/64	Drewry's Bluff	−0.06	0.08

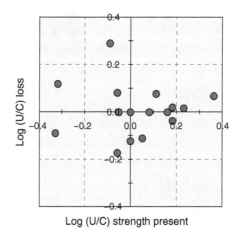

Figure 1 Variation of the ratio of Union/Confederate losses with the ratio of Union/Confederate strengths present

with the result that some units might not arrive until the battle was virtually over. He also noted that, even when the larger army had been fully assembled, there were tactical difficulties in bringing its superior numbers into action. Regiments in the rear were blocked by troops in the firing line and regiments on the flanks had to advance with due caution and wheel inward before their fire could be effective; before that manoeuvre could be accomplished, the outnumbered force had often observed the potential threat and had made a timely retreat. Kirkpatrick suggested that these reasons explained why the advantage of having superior numbers in the ACW appeared to be smaller than expected from Lanchester's Square Law.

A later review (Eccles 1999) of these various attempts to validate Lanchester's models concluded that the ratio of the strengths of the opposing forces was probably an important factor in determining the ratio of casualties inflicted, but that there were many other factors which could be even more important. Nearly a century after the publication of Lanchester's combat models, no analysis had defined a clear relationship between loss ratios and strength ratios. But, despite the lack of any statistical support for Lanchester's Square Law, it continued to be cited by those who were guided by faith rather than by evidence.

6 Features of the American Civil War 1861–1865

6.1 Suitability for this Analysis

The American Civil War (ACW) is particularly suitable for a quantitative study because the armies engaged were relatively homogeneous. The dominant arm in any ACW army was the infantry, which generally constituted about 80 per cent of an army's strength (Underwood 1887) and inflicted around 85 per cent of the enemy army's losses (McPherson 1982). In this war, cavalry played a very minor role on the battlefield, and was principally used for raids and reconnaissance; hence battle losses were caused almost exclusively by firepower (in accordance with the assumptions inherent in Lanchester's Square Law) and were rarely distorted by the shock action of mounted cavalry. Artillery generally inflicted 10 per cent (Dupuy 1985, p. 8) of the enemy army's losses (or more in exceptionally favourable circumstances), but since the number of guns was closely related to the number of infantry (normally about 3 per 1,000) the fighting strength of an ACW army may credibly be represented by the total number of soldiers present for duty. Since most of the losses in an ACW battle were inflicted during infantry firefights, it is reasonable to expect them to accord with Lanchester's Square Law.

The ACW is also suitable for a quantitative study because it featured a relatively large number of open-field battles between the opposing armies of the Union and the Confederacy. Many of the other wars in the eighteenth and nineteenth centuries were shorter, or featured more manoeuvring and sieges than battles, or involved several different national armies with varying capabilities.

Furthermore, the ACW has been intensively studied and there is a multitude of reasonably consistent published data on the numbers and losses of the troops involved in many of the major battles (although in the final months of the war the Confederacy's record-keeping deteriorated and the data on its armies in that period are scanty). Soon after the war, a study (Livermore 1901) estimated the numbers and losses in those battles where the casualties in one or other of the opposing armies exceeded 1,000, thus excluding smaller combats which can be affected by particular local circumstances or topography. In subsequent years, additional data has appeared in a multitude of histories (notably those by Foote 1963, Davis 1983 and McPherson 1988), in the personnel recollections of participants (Underwood 1887) and in battlefield guides (Kennedy 1990).

The reported losses in an ACW battle were generally classified as killed, wounded and missing; the last category included prisoners, deserters and stragglers, all of whom might have been wounded or unwounded. The proportion of missing in ACW battles was generally smaller than in earlier wars because ACW cavalry could not sustain an effectively destructive pursuit. For some battles, the data on losses are incomplete, either because not all units in the opposing armies submitted post-battle returns of losses, or because sympathetic commanders were reluctant to label as 'missing' some absentees who might simply have straggled temporarily to forage for food and clothing, or to recuperate from the trauma of battle. In all such cases, Livermore used his best judgement to arrive at credible approximations of the armies' losses. Some of the wounded and the missing rejoined their units after a few days and so were not permanently deducted from the strength of their armies; however it is impractical to distinguish between permanent and temporary losses, and this analysis uses the reported losses = killed + wounded + missing.

Thus the ACW is a uniquely favourable test case for the analysis of the effect of superior numbers because it features largely homogenous forces, many open field battles, and relatively good data on numbers and losses. However, in such an analysis it is important to understand that the outcomes of ACW battles could be affected by the various other factors discussed in the following Section, as well as by superior numbers.

6.2 Factors Relevant to the Outcomes of ACW battles

The **leadership** qualities of the army commanders in the ACW varied considerably. Some were well-trained professional soldiers who rose to the challenge of infinitely greater responsibilities than they had experienced in peacetime. Others were civilian amateurs who quickly learned new skills. Yet others (from military, civilian or political backgrounds) achieved promotion to senior ranks through nepotism or political influence, but had limitations which in normal circumstances would have disqualified them from high command. The outcome of any particular battle could be affected by the relative competence of the opposing commanders.

The Confederate and Union infantry were both equipped with a mixture of muzzle-loading **firearms**, including modern muzzle-loading rifles (Springfield and Enfield), second-rate rifles and smoothbore muskets. In the battles considered in this analysis, the proportion of troops equipped with modern rifles increased (roughly in parallel) as the war went on, but in any particular battle the Confederate army was likely to have a smaller proportion of modern rifles. Accordingly, it is reasonable to assume that the Confederates had a small but reasonably consistent disadvantage in the performance of their infantry firearms. The disadvantage was probably greatest in the first year of the war, when some Confederate forces were very poorly equipped. In the latter years of the war, some Union cavalry units were equipped with Spencer and other types of repeating rifles: a brigade-level combat at Hoover's Gap in 1863 suggested that a Spencer rifle was at least twice as effective on the battlefield as a muzzle-loading rifle, but there were never sufficient repeating rifles in the Union army to affect significantly the outcome of a major battle.

The Confederate and Union armies used a mixture of smoothbore and more-modern rifled **artillery**, with the Union army having the larger proportion of the more modern rifled types. The relative effectiveness of these two types, and the effectiveness of artillery relative to infantry, depended on the topography of the battlefield. Union artillery was very effective at Malvern Hill and at Gettysburg where it had a good field of fire and could direct convergent salvos against attacking Confederate infantry, but was much less effective in the tangled scrub of the Wilderness.

Soldiers who had good **training** and had previous **experience** in battle were inevitably more effective in combat than raw recruits, however well-motivated. At the start of the ACW both the Union and Confederate armies were formed from poorly trained and inexperienced volunteers (Lincoln said that they 'were all green together'). In some Union armies there were a few units from the pre-war US regular army which generally stayed loyal to the Union; these units retained their regular-army qualities. Both armies improved their competence as the war went on, though within an army the effectiveness of its individual regiments could vary considerably.

On rare occasions (such as Chancellorsville and Cedar Creek) a careless army was taken by **surprise** by the timing or direction of an enemy attack. In such cases, the careless army sustained disproportionate losses until it could be organised and deployed to engage the enemy effectively.

It is evident from any study of ACW battle data that the losses in killed and wounded sustained by troops attacking long-prepared or even improvised **fortifications** were much higher than those of the defenders, and, as the war went on, experienced troops fortified their positions whenever time permitted. In assaults on fortified lines, the relative losses in the opposing armies depended principally on the strength of the fortifications rather than on the numbers of the soldiers engaged. In such assaults, the effectiveness of each individual defender was several times greater than that of each attacker: in the ACW it was considered (Fuller 1958, p. 62) that one rifleman in a trench was worth five in front of it and battle data show that the defender/attacker effectiveness ratios often exceeded 10:1. Half a century later in World War I, when fortifications were much more sophisticated, the defender/attacker effectiveness ratio could be almost as high as 100:1. It was therefore appropriate to exclude from this analysis, which is focussed on the effect of the relative strengths of the opposing armies, the outcomes of assaults on fortified lines.

The battles of the ACW were fought in varied **terrain**, including farmland, forest and scrub. Thick scrub (as was found in the Wilderness area of Virginia) inhibited the movement of troops off the few roads and trails, and also limited the scope for converging fire, thus reducing the value of superior numbers. It was advantageous for an army whenever possible to occupy high ground (such as Hazel Grove and Cemetery Hill) which gave its artillery a good field of fire, and to deploy its infantry behind a stone wall which gave it some protection from enemy fire. Such local terrain features influenced the results of low-level engagements but rarely determined the outcomes of major battles.

Both the Union and the Confederate armies were initially composed of volunteers who had high **morale** because both believed that they were fighting in a just cause and because they had not yet endured uncomfortable deprivations and high casualties. Later in the war, both armies were diluted with unwilling conscripts and their morale fluctuated with the popularity and success/failure of successive generals, but morale remained high enough in both Union and Confederate armies to sustain determined attacks into heavy fire through most of the war. In battles fought in the final few months of the war, both armies contained growing proportions of unenthusiastic conscripts who appear to have made the (dubious) decision that an enemy prison camp would be safer than continued front-line service, and were thus willing to surrender in larger numbers than was usual earlier in the war. Confederate data on numbers and losses for this period are generally inadequate, so the 1865 battles (which may have been affected by declining morale in both Union and Confederate armies) have been excluded from the analysis.

The outcome of any ACW battle depended to varying degrees on the relative strengths of the armies involved **and also** on the other factors discussed in Section 6.2. In some battles, one or more of these other factors (such as fortifications) were dominant, and their impact overshadowed the effect of superior numbers. Since this analysis sought to illuminate the effect of superior numbers, and to discover if that effect in ACW battles was in accordance with Lanchester's Square Law, the battles in which other factors were important have been excluded from this analysis.

If Lanchester's Square Law model is valid, the ratio of Union/Confederate losses in ACW battles included in this analysis should be inversely proportional to the ratio of Union/Confederate numbers, in accordance with equation (2). But the outcomes of the battles which have been included were inevitably affected to various minor degrees by the other factors discussed previously, as well as by the relative strength of the opposing armies, and consequently it is reasonable to expect that the battles outcomes are scattered around the linear trend line predicted by equation (7).

7 Study of the Battles of the American Civil War

Unfortunately for the studies by Weiss and Kirkpatrick (cited in Section 5.5), much of Livermore's data on numbers and losses in the ACW are not entirely suitable for an assessment of Lanchester's Square Law; it needs to be reviewed rigorously, and in some cases must be amended to accord with recent research.

1. In some cases, the losses of a defeated army were underestimated by its commander either because not all of its units submitted post-battle reports, or because the commander wished to downplay the scale of his army's defeat (after Pea Ridge General Van Dorn estimated his army's losses at 800, but modern research suggests that they were at least double that number).
2. The estimated strength of an army on the battlefield sometimes failed to take full account of the straggling by tired, hungry or ill-equipped troops (in the 1862 Maryland campaign the Confederate army was depleted by thousands of stragglers who were shoeless, exhausted by the preceding onerous campaign, or had moral objections to fighting on Northern soil).
3. The estimated strength of an ACW army on the battlefield sometimes, in the early stages of the war, included troops who had no firearms (like some Confederate units at Wilson's Creek), and often included troops which did not come into action (like the Union Fifth Army Corps at Antietam where a quarter of the Union army was not actually engaged).

These problems were addressed in this analysis by amending some of Livermore's data to accord with modern research, and to reflect the number of troops who were actively engaged and thereby contributed to the outcome of the battle. This was done only for battles where the amendment significantly altered the strength or loss ratios by more than the uncertainty inherent in all historical data.

In addition, Livermore's data for some battles (like Shiloh, Fair Oaks, Chancellorsville and Gettysburg) combined several discrete engagements which were actually separate in time and/or space and which featured different strength and loss ratios. In prolonged battles during which one or both of the opposing armies received substantial reinforcements, Livermore's data on the total number of troops present seriously misrepresents the number actively engaged at any particular time. This problem was addressed in this analysis (wherever there is sufficient information in detailed histories) by disaggregating some of Livermore's battles to identify discrete phases or sectors for which credible strength and loss ratios could be estimated. This analysis considered separately the engagements at Fair Oaks and Seven Pines which were both fought 31 May 1862, and considered separately the first day of the battle of Shiloh after which the Union army received substantial reinforcements overnight.

Lanchester's combat models assumed that all of the fighting units in the opposing forces were able to engage the enemy effectively. Thus an assessment of the validity of his Square Law by analysis of ACW battles should be made in terms of the strengths of the armies which were actually engaged, omitting unarmed troops, uncommitted reserves and horse-holders. In a few battles, the strength of one or both armies varied considerably when substantial reinforcements arrived near the end (for example, at Cedar Mountain) and consequently had a limited effect on the outcome. Whenever the chronological battle narrative provided sufficient detail, this analysis estimated the time-averaged strength of the relevant army. If the narrative was inadequate, the strength of the reinforcements was halved to derive an approximate estimate of the strength of the relevant army and hence a representative strength ratio of opposing troops engaged (as discussed in Appendix 1 where appropriate).

Lanchester's combat models took no account of diseconomies of scale. In a few ACW scenarios, the Union/Confederate initial strength ratios were particularly large or particularly small, and the smaller army chose to fight rather than retreat. In these exceptional cases, it was impractical for all of the larger army to engage the enemy effectively, because it was inevitable that the larger army would take longer to deploy than the smaller. Even when the larger army had been fully assembled on the battlefield, some of its infantry regiments would either be behind their army's front line where they could not see the enemy or on the flank and beyond the range of their rifled muskets; in neither case could these regiments engage the enemy effectively. Hence not all of the troops present in the larger army were effectively engaged. Furthermore the ratio of troops engaged varied through the battle and the time-averaged ratio was less than the ratio of total troops engaged. In a meeting engagement, for example, the ratio of strength engaged was probably about unity when the leading units first went into action; later, as both armies deployed, the ratio would rise progressively towards the ratio of the numbers engaged, and would then fall as the outnumbered army retreated. For each such battle, where there was no chronological narrative, the time-averaged ratio of strength engaged was estimated by reducing the strength of the larger army by one third of its numerical superiority (for example, in a battle where the ratio of troops present was 2:1, this analysis assumed that the time-averaged ratio of troops engaged was 1.67:1). This assumption yielded ratios which were uncertain but which were more credible than assuming that the troops providing numerical superiority should be considered as having either full effectiveness or zero effectiveness; an alternative assumption for these few battles would not alter the overall trend of the battle data.

This methodology for amending some of Livermore's data, plus the addition of some data from other data-books, histories and battlefield guides, yielded strength ratios and loss ratios for twenty-eight discrete open-field battles where the outcomes could be expected to follow Lanchester's Square Law. These ratios are presented in Table 2 and discussed in Appendix 1.

Figure 2 presents the Union/Confederate loss ratios plotted against the corresponding Union/Confederate ratios of strength engaged. Most of the data points are reasonably close, given the uncertainty involved in deriving U/C ratios of strength engaged and of losses, to the line sloping at 45 degrees which represents the prediction of Lanchester's Square Law. The data points are scattered above and below the trend line, reflecting variations in the circumstances of each battle. Some of the plotted ratios for individual battles are disputable, particularly for those battles which are poorly documented and for those where a representative strength ratio has been derived using the author's judgment. However it is clear that the Union/Confederate loss ratio declines significantly as the Union/Confederate strength ratio of troops engaged increases, roughly in accordance with Lanchester's Square Law.

The two outliers (Fair Oaks and Malvern Hill) were battles in which the Union army had clear superiority in artillery. Ideally this superiority might (in a more-detailed analysis) be reflected in the strength ratios of the opposing armies. For example, it is believed that at Malvern Hill the Union artillery inflicted half of the Confederate casualties (Sears 1992, p. 332) so it would be reasonable to plot that particular battle outcome at about double its strength ratio, which would be very close to the trend line.

Table 2 Revised data on numbers and losses in ACW battles

Date	Battle	Log U/C strength engaged	Log U/C loss	Log C/U effectiveness
21/06/61	First Bull Run	0	0.137	+0.137
10/08/61	Wilson's Creek	−0.097	0.033	−0.064
06/04/62	Shiloh	−0.027	0.033	+0.066
05/05/62	Fort Magruder	−0.097	0.270	+0.175
31/05/62	Seven Pines	−0.071	−0.046	−0.117
31/05/62	Fair Oaks	0.148	−0.432	−0.284
01/06/62	Orchard Station	0.114	0.013	+0.127
30/06/62	Glendale	0.182	−0.071	+0.111
01/07/62	Malvern Hill	0	−0.275	−0.275
09/08/62	Cedar Mountain	−0.113	0.225	+0.112
28/08/62	Groveton	−0.154	−0.018	−0.172
14/09/62	Turner's Gap	0.204	−0.125	+0.079
17/09/62	Antietam	0.146	0.079	+0.225
06/10/62	Perryville	0.161	0.093	+0.250
07/12/62	Prairie Grove	0.045	−0.022	+0.023
13/12/62	Fredricksburg, Prospect Hill	−0.126	0.122	−0.004
31/12/62	Stone's River	0.092	0.052	+0.144
03/05/63	Chancellorsville, Fairview salient	0	−0.018	−0.018
16/05/63	Champion Hill	0.187	−0.201	−0.014
01/07/63	Gettysburg, North and West	−0.108	0.146	+0.038
02/07/63	Gettysburg, Peach Orchard etc.	0	0.176	+0.176
20/09/63	Chickamauga	−0.065	−0.041	−0.105
08/04/64	Mansfield	−0.222	0.348	+0.126
09/04/64	Pleasant Hill	−0.014	−0.077	−0.091
16/05/64	Drewry Bluff	−0.057	0.220	+0.163
05/06/64	Piedmont	0.243	−0.260	−0.017
09/06/64	Monocacy	−0.112	0.212	+0.100
22/09/64	Fisher's Hill	0.376	−0.366	+0.010
	Average of 28			+0.032

This analysis focussed wherever practicable on the ratio of the opposing forces engaged in a battle rather than on the ratio of those present. Generally these ratios are similar, but, in some battles, part of one of the opposing forces

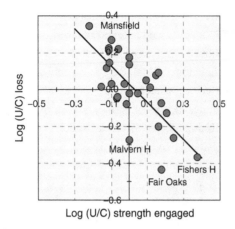

Figure 2 Variation of the ratio of Union/Confederate losses with the ratio of Union/Confederate strengths engaged

did not engage either because that commander failed to direct his forces effectively or because he retained a reserve in idleness until the battle was over. Prudent commanders have always tried to retain a reserve so that they can react to any unexpected development during a battle, but the reserve should be engaged before the end of the battle (either to mitigate the consequences of a defeat, or to make a victory even more decisive) otherwise its strength would be wasted. The effective engagement of the French reserve at Borodino or of the Union reserve at Antietam would probably have yielded decisive victories in those battles, with potentially significant effects of the associated campaigns.

The right-hand column of Table 2 shows the Confederate/Union ratio of the soldiers' individual effectiveness in each battle. In successive battles between the same opposing armies, Lanchester's Square Law suggests that this ratio should be constant, but in practice it is scattered because of the particular circumstances of each battle (leadership, terrain, etc., as discussed in Section 6). The average ratio suggests that there was no significant difference between the individual effectiveness of Union and Confederate soldiers. In this analysis, as noted in Section 3.2, 'individual effectiveness' is an all-embracing measure, combining weapon performance, enemy vulnerability and all other factors which affect battle outcomes apart from superior numbers.

It has been claimed (McWhiney 1982) that in ACW battles the attacking army was at a disadvantage, and that the Confederacy lost the ACW because its armies attacked too often. This is a plausible hypothesis because ACW artillery was more effective at close range, and therefore offered more support to defenders than attackers. In some of the battles considered in this analysis, the opposing armies both attacked and counter-attacked in different phases of the battle. However, in about a dozen cases, one army was mostly on the attack and the other was mostly defending. When the Union armies attacked, the battle data suggests that the Confederates had a greater individual effectiveness. When the Confederate armies attacked, the battle data are more variable, ranging from success at Perryville through mixed fortune at Shiloh to disaster at Malvern Hill. It may be concluded that offensive tactics could be successful if the attacks were well-planned or lucky, and defensive tactics could be successful if the enemy obliged by attacking imprudently.

This Section has established that the Union/Confederate loss ratios in open-field battles of the ACW were (roughly) inversely proportional to the Union/ Confederate ratios of forces engaged, in accordance with Lanchester's Square Law. This is the **first** analysis in open literature to show that his Square Law was approximately correct for (virtually) homogeneous forces, provided that it is correctly interpreted in terms of those forces which are actually engaged and which are capable of inflicting losses on the enemy rather than in terms of all forces on or near the battlefield. This emphasis on forces actually engaged highlights the importance (in the ACW and throughout military history) of the non-combat elements which ensure that all of the combat elements of a military force are brought into action. These non-combat elements should provide:

- good reconnaissance of the force's area of operations,
- decisive and rapid command and control to avoid dangers and exploit opportunities,
- reliable and quick communications to direct subordinate fighting units,
- mobility to facilitate fast and effective redeployment and thus ensure that all of the fighting units could participate in a forthcoming battle, and
- logistic support to supply the fighting units during a battle.

In the German army of the twentieth century, the Prussian generals often displayed an aristocratic disdain for the non-combat elements (such as logistics, signals and intelligence), and this cultural flaw (Macksey 2006, p. 37) fatally limited that army's ability to transform its tactical successes into strategic victories (in 1914 and 1941).

Any general model intended to predict the loss ratio in an ACW battle would have to include the effects of the following factors:

- *superior numbers* – the U/C loss ratio could be estimated as inversely proportional to the initial U/C strength ratio, so that doubling the strength of the Union army would halve the U/C loss ratio,

- *fortification* – improvised ACW field fortifications typically increased the strength of the defenders by a factor of between 2 and 5, or by a much larger factor for pre-prepared fortifications,
- *leadership* – Napoleon's contemporaries judged that his presence was worth 40,000 men on the battlefield, thus increasing the strength of a typical Napoleonic army by half; some ACW commanders were similarly talented and inspirational, so the model should include a factor based on a comparison of the opposing commanders,
- *artillery* – a dominant array of guns could double the strength of the defenders, and
- *surprise and training* – these factors should be included in any model of the ACW, but there are insufficient data to estimate their scale.

Generally there are no significant disparities in the *firepower* or *morale* in the opposing armies in the ACW, but these factors would have to be included in a combat model applicable to other wars.

8 Evidence from Wars before the ACW

8.1 Difficulties in Validation

On the battlefields of the ACW, infantry armed with rifled muskets were dominant; artillery played a minor role (except on those few occasions when the terrain was particularly favourable) and cavalry charges were almost invariably costly and ineffective. But in the wars of the eighteenth and early nineteenth centuries, the infantry had smoothbore muskets with inferior range and accuracy, so artillery and cavalry played more important roles. Napoleon famously used massed batteries of artillery to deplete and demoralise enemy troops at his chosen point of attack. Cavalry were generally impotent against well-trained infantry formed in square, but could be devastatingly destructive of infantry which was demoralised, disordered or surprised in a vulnerable formation; the results of some battles in this period were significantly affected by successful cavalry charges. Furthermore, an army which lacked sufficient good cavalry was at an appreciable disadvantage because the clear and present threat from enemy cavalry forced its infantry to move and deploy with great caution on any battlefield. After a battle, the cavalry of the victorious army could undertake vigorous pursuit to capture many prisoners, artillery and supplies and to turn the defeated army's retreat into a disorderly rout. Consequently, the combat power of an army in this period should ideally be represented by three numbers defining its interdependent infantry, cavalry and artillery (like land, labour and capital in a national economy) rather than by a single number which could reasonably represent the combat power of an army in the ACW.

Analysis of battles in the eighteenth and early nineteenth centuries presents even greater difficulties than the analysis of battles in the ACW. In the earlier wars, it is even more difficult to estimate the numbers of troops present in the opposing armies, the numbers which engaged and the losses they suffered. In these wars, an army's losses might be caused by an enemy cavalry charge or might be inflated by prisoners/missing lost during a disorderly and hard-pressed retreat, rather than by the firepower modelled by Lanchester. In several of these wars, armies included various allied contingents with different levels of performance and motivation, and also included substantial contingents of irregular troops (such as Croats and Cossacks) which were useful for skirmishing and reconnaissance, but were of limited value in a major battle,

It follows that any Lanchester-focussed analysis must identify specific periods of warfare in which opposing armies with reasonably consistent qualities fought sufficient battles to form an adequate database, and must expect that loss ratios may be distorted by the impact of cavalry charges and/or of losses in retreats (neither of which are represented in Lanchester's model).

There were several wars in the first half of the eighteenth century, but most of them were short and involved more sieges and manoeuvres than battles. The Great Northern War in 1700–21, and the War of Spanish Succession in 1701–14, each involved about a dozen battles but these battles included several combinations of different national forces, and many of the outcomes were affected by field fortifications or cavalry charges. Neither war yielded a database suitable for this analysis.

8.2 Seven Years War, 1756–1763

Although most wars in the eighteenth century are unsuitable for analysis (featuring commanders and armies of very variable quality), the Seven Years War is an exception. In this war, the Prussian armies were vastly outnumbered by the armies of Austria, France and Russia, and Frederick the Great could only assure Prussia's survival by accepting battle at unfavourable odds against individual allied armies. In such battles, he relied on his own leadership and the quality of his troops to win a decisive victory which would put one ally out of action (at least temporarily) while he moved against the others. He generally sought victory by a tactical manoeuvre to outflank the opposing army and attack it advantageously. If this manoeuvre was successful (as at Leuthen), Frederick achieved a favourable loss ratio, but if it failed (because the flank march was disordered by terrain or because the enemy redeployed), the loss ratio was unfavourable to the Prussians. In some of the battles in the Seven Years War (notably Rossbach), cavalry played a decisive role, and the timing and bravery of the decisive cavalry charge was more important than the overall numbers involved in those battles. In some battles, the losses of the defeated army included a large proportion of prisoners/ missing, and it is generally unclear whether these losses were incurred during the battle or during the subsequent retreat (when such losses could be attributed to the demoralisation of the defeated army rather than to the firepower of the victors). In such cases, this analysis adopted an arbitrary but consistent compromise and assumed that half of the losses in prisoners/missing were incurred during the battle.

In this war, the Prussians fought one major battle against the French, four against the Russians and eight against the Austrians, of which one (Breslau in 1757) featured assault on a fortified camp and is accordingly excluded. The remaining seven battles against the Austrians form a (barely) adequate database. The plotted results of these seven battles (see Appendix 2) suggest that the Prussian/Austrian loss ratio decreases as the Prussian/Austrian strength ratio increases, broadly in accordance with the Square Law, but the results are considerably scattered. Leuthen is an outlier, with a loss ratio particularly favourable to the Prussians.

8.3 War of American Independence, 1775–1783

The battles of the War of American Independence were decided primarily by infantry firefights, because much of the terrain was unsuitable for the large-scale deployment of cavalry and artillery. Both of the rival armies were heterogeneous and included contingents with very different levels of motivation and combat capability. The various Royal armies included British regulars, German mercenaries, American loyalists, Canadians and Indians. The rebel armies included various proportions of disciplined Continentals, elite volunteers (such as Morgan's riflemen) and sometimes-fragile militia. There is considerable doubt about the strengths of the rival armies present at the various battles, and about how their strengths varied during the battles as various contingents arrived or fled. There were exceptionally high losses in some battles because defeated troops, wounded or unwounded, appear to have surrendered in large numbers (at Bennington, Camden and Cowpens). For all of these reasons, this war was considered to be unsuitable for this analysis.

8.4 Wars of the French Revolution, 1792–1802

The new French Republic fought many battles in this period against coalitions of counter-revolutionary forces. However there is extreme uncertainty about the strength ratios and loss ratios in these battles, and the performance of the French Revolutionary armies varied dramatically with their morale which was in turn dependent on their training, armament and supply (all often inadequate) and on the charisma of their leaders. Fragile morale led to some demoralised routs. Furthermore, the performance of these revolutionary armies improved progressively through this decade as the troops accumulated training and experience, and as talented young officers (like General Bonaparte) were promoted to command. The lack of reliable data, and the wide variations in the effectiveness of revolutionary armies, make this series of wars unsuitable for this analysis.

8.5 Wars of the first Grande Armee, 1805–1807

The Napoleonic wars were fought between the armies of the French Empire and its allies and the armies of almost every other European nation. The military effectiveness of some European national armies varied through the period 1805–15, as they introduced successive reforms while the French armies deteriorated after their losses (notably in Russia in 1812). It is therefore necessary to analyse the Napoleonic wars separately, to identify those in which the relative effectiveness of the opposing armies may be presumed to be (broadly) consistent and which are therefore suitable for this analysis.

In the 1805–7 period, the principal French army (the Grande Armee) was formed from the troops which had been intensively trained in the camps around Boulogne in the two preceding years. This army was an outstandingly effective organisation with well-motivated and competent troops, with field officers and general officers promoted on merit, and with the Emperor Napoleon as its exceptionally talented commander. It outclassed its Austrian, Prussian and Russian opponents, whose armies all were poorly organised and commanded. There is considerable variation between different historical estimates of the strength ratios and loss ratios in some of the battles within this period. In others, the opposing armies received reinforcements during the fighting and this analysis had to derive representative strength ratios. In two battles (Austerlitz and Jena) the numbers of prisoners/missing from the defeated armies were exceptionally large; in both of these cases it was assumed (as in Section 8.2) that half of these losses were incurred during the pursuit of the defeated army and hence were not attributable to the enemy's firepower. The results of the eight battles which had credible data, and did not involve fortifications or street fighting, suggest (see Appendix 3) that the French/Allied loss ratio decreased as the French/Allied strength ratio increased, broadly in accordance with Lanchester's Square Law. The results also suggest that the individual effectiveness of French soldiers was about double that of their opponents in this period.

8.6 Peninsular War in Spain and Portugal, 1808–1813

The French forces which fought in the Iberian Peninsula in 1808–13 included veteran corps detached from the ever-victorious Grande Armee, improvised units of French conscripts without previous experience and foreign contingents of varying capability. The Spanish armies which opposed the French invasion were often poorly armed, ill-trained and ineptly commanded; they generally lacked effective cavalry and were prone to collapse under pressure. Accordingly, the outcomes of Franco-Spanish battles varied very considerably and are thus unsuitable for this analysis. The battles between the French and British armies, which in the latter years of this war incorporated Portugese and Spanish contingents, have been well documented by historians, and there are reasonably good data on the strength and loss ratios in eight battles (see data sources in Appendix 4). Excluding Bussaco, where the British had an untypical advantage of terrain, the data on the remaining seven battles (see Appendix 4) suggest that the French/British loss ratio declined as the French/British strength ratio increased, broadly in accordance with Lanchester's Square Law. The data suggest that the individual effectiveness of the British soldiers was nearly double that of the French.

8.7 Napoleon's wars against Austria in 1809 and Russia in 1812

In preparing for these wars, the French army was diluted with drafts of inexperienced French conscripts and by allied contingents, and the resulting mixture inevitably fell below the standards of the 1805–7 Grande Armee. Similarly, the Austrian and Russian armies incorporated increasing numbers of poorly trained militia as the wars went on. The uneven quality of the opposing armies probably affected battle outcomes and blurred the effect of superior numbers.

Neither of these wars had sufficient battles to form an adequate database. The 1809 war lasted only three months. In 1812, the Russians prudently retreated before Napoleon's huge army, fighting only a few rear-guard actions until their own forces had united and Napoleon's had been depleted by weather and logistics. Furthermore, the quoted strength and loss ratios for the battles in Russia vary considerably between different histories; contemporary estimates of the French/Russian loss ratio at the important battle of Borodino, for example, varied from 0.2 to 1.6, and a consensus of 0.7 has been reached only after the fall of the Soviet Union. Accordingly, these two wars are unsuitable for this analysis.

8.8 Napoleon's Last Campaign in Germany, 1813

The 1813 campaign, following the destruction in Russia of most of the Grande Armee of 1812, was fought in Germany. Napoleon's army had to be reconstructed largely from poorly trained and inexperienced conscripts, and was notably deficient in cavalry. Similarly the Russian army had to incorporate many new recruits to replace its considerable 1812 losses, and the Prussian and Austrian armies had to be rebuilt after their defeats in 1806 and 1809 and the consequent draconian terms of peace (loss of territory, indemnities and limits on their forces) imposed by the victorious French. The strength ratios for many of the battles in this campaign were ill-defined, because the opposing forces were continually depleted by casualties, sickness, straggling and desertion, and were periodically augmented by reinforcements. In this campaign, inexperienced troops in a bad situation tended to surrender or desert in large numbers, and most of those prisoners/missing were only indirectly victims of enemy firepower; some battles where the proportion of prisoners/missing was particularly large (and hence distorted the loss ratios) have been omitted from this analysis. But there are sufficient battles in 1813 where the strength and loss ratios are reasonably robust and unaffected by special circumstances to provide an acceptable database (see Appendix 5).

The results of the battles in the 1813 are scattered because the opposing armies were all heterogeneous and included veterans, conscripts and militia with differing capabilities, But the battle data are broadly consistent with Lanchester's Square Law, and suggest that the individual effectiveness of the Allied troops was slightly greater than that of the French.

8.9 Napoleon at Bay, 1814

Napoleon's losses in 1813 were almost as disastrous as in 1812 and he struggled to raise yet another new and inexperienced army to defend eastern France from much larger Allied armies during the first few months of 1814. There were too few battles in these months, and the data on strengths and losses are generally too uncertain, to form an adequate database.

8.10 Synopsis

Not all of the wars in this period were suitable for analysis on the effect of superior numbers because the armies were more heterogeneous than those in the ACW, because cavalry and artillery played more important roles, and because the data on the armies' numbers and losses are more uncertain. But in four wars there were sufficient credible data to suggest that the battle outcomes were broadly consistent with Lanchester's Square Law (see Appendices 2 to 5).

9 Evidence from Wars after the ACW

9.1 Obstacles to Validation

The other major wars in the nineteenth century were all affected by the rapid developments in weaponry such as rifled muskets, breech-loading and repeating rifles, rifled and breech-loading artillery and machine guns. Each successive innovation yielded longer range and/or improved accuracy and/or more-rapid fire, which together provided greater firepower. In this period, any army which lagged in the adoption of new weapons or in the evolution of tactical doctrine was likely to suffer disproportionately heavy losses. It follows that battle data from each war, employing a particular array of weaponry, must be analysed separately. Unfortunately for this analysis, the mid-nineteenth-century wars were all relatively short, and the Crimean War 1853–6, the Franco-Austrian War 1859 and the Schleswig-Holstein War 1864 involved only a few major battles between the opposing armies (and in some of those the outcome was distorted by special circumstances). Accordingly, these three wars do not provide useful evidence on the importance of superior numbers, though the outcome of the open-field battle of the Alma in the Crimea did demonstrate the superiority of the Allies' rifled muskets over the Russians' smoothbores. In the Russo-Turkish War 1877, the second Boer War 1899–1902 and the Russo-Japanese War 1904–5 there were few battles and most of their outcomes were affected by the strength of field or permanent fortifications (sometimes incorporating barbed wire), so they are also unsuitable for analysis. However it seemed possible that analysis of the two 'Wars of German Unification' in 1866 and 1870–1 would yield useful results.

9.2 Seven Weeks War, 1866

In 1866, the Austrians and Prussians fought five corps-level battles along the frontier and one decisive battle (Koniggratz/Sadowa) between the main armies of the opposing nations. In all of these few battles, the strength ratio of the troops engaged was close to unity, so the loss ratios in those battles do not reflect the effect of superior numbers (see Appendix 6) and hence do not clearly reflect the importance of superior numbers, but they are reasonably consistent with Lanchester's Square Law. The individual effectiveness of a Prussian soldier appears to have been some five times greater than an Austrian, arising from the superiority of the Prussians' breech-loading rifles, tactical doctrine and leadership.

9.3 Franco-Prussian War, 1870–1871

In the summer of 1870, the Prussians and their German allies fought seven battles against the soldiers of the Second French Empire (and subsequently fought more battles against the improvised armies of the French Republic, which yielded variable results reflecting their disparate composition and armament and are thus unsuitable for this analysis). The results of two battles were affected by fortifications and the result of another (Sedan) was largely determined by the grossly unfavourable position of the Imperial French army, described by one of its generals as 'in a chamber pot'. The remaining four are too few to form an adequate database (see Appendix 7), but they suggest that the French soldiers had an individual effectiveness which was significantly higher (about 30 per cent) than the Germans. The Imperial French soldiers had better rifles than the Prussians but this advantage was offset by the Prussians' larger numbers, superior artillery and better leadership, so they won the campaign.

9.4 Synopsis

Analysis of these two wars showed that neither of them had sufficient open-field battles to provide an adequate database for the validation of Lanchester's Square Law. However, the battle outcomes are very relevant to the over-arching debate about quality versus quantity. The heavy Austrian losses in 1866 showed their errors of failing to invest in a breech-loading rifle and of relying on bayonet charges. In 1870, the French had good rifles but poor artillery. The Austrian and the French were both bedevilled by poor staff work and by fractious relationships amongst senior officers. Sections 7 and 8 show that superior numbers can deliver victory, *ceteris paribus*, but Section 9 shows that the effect of superior numbers can be overshadowed by disparities in weaponry, tactical doctrine and leadership.

10 The Influence of Lanchester's Square Law (?)

Despite its limitations, the Square Law model has proved enduringly attractive because of its seductive simplicity (like many similarly unsubstantiated axioms in economics and other social sciences) and because its emphasis on superior numbers apparently provided mathematical justification for a traditional military maxim enshrined by Napoleon and reflecting the conditions of combat in his period. Lanchester's emphasis on the importance of superior numbers was aligned with the pre-1914 views of Colonel (later Marshal) Foch and the French Ecole de Guerre that infantry charges could succeed by sheer weight of numbers at the critical sector of the front. It has been tempting for credulous politicians to believe that there was some enduring and inherent virtue in having superior numbers, and to be over-impressed by the sheer scale of military forces (such as the 'Russian steam-roller' in the years before 1914) without paying enough attention to their quality. This belief has been especially prevalent among the leaders of popular revolutions (such as Jefferson in America, Carnot in France and Stalin in Russia) who were ideologically attracted to the concept of a people in arms. Such leaders have not always recognised that the quality of a military force can offset the effect of superior numbers. In fact, it is doubtful that there are any examples in modern military history where an army or navy with inferior weaponry has achieved victory by virtue of superior numbers alone. But there are many contrary examples where a better-led or a better-armed force has triumphed against heavy odds (such as at Leuthen, Auerstadt and Chancellorsville, as well as in imperialist battles at Aragee, Ulundi and Omdurman).

The Square Law hypothesis remained, through the twentieth century, attractive to those politicians who deplored the rapid and apparently inexorable rise through the twentieth century in the unit cost of successive generations of many classes of military equipment, and the associated shrinkage of national armed forces in the UK and elsewhere. Faith in numbers rather than quality allowed these politicians to hope that their nation might avoid the substantial costs and daunting technological risks of advanced modern projects by procuring a larger number of less-effective weapon systems. Concern about the shrinkage of national armed forces was shared by some senior military officers, partly perhaps out of cap-badge loyalty but mostly from an instinctive antipathy to being outnumbered.

Most military planning of force development and operational strategy is done behind closed doors, so it is difficult to identify unambiguous examples of distortions arising from a misplaced belief in Lanchester's Square Law and an associated blind faith in superior numbers.

- In 1914, Germany's leaders were prepared to risk a preventative war with Russia because they feared the disparity between Russian and German population growth (the former was growing twice as fast) and the associated expansion of the Russian army. In fact, the myth of the 'Russian steamroller' was demolished at Tannenberg only a month after the start of World War I.
- Mussolini, in 1936, cited eight million bayonets as an indicator of Italian military power, despite the fact that his army's armoured fighting vehicles (AFV) were sub-standard.
- In the late 1930s, the French Army rejected Major de Gaulle's argument in favour of an elite professional army built around several armoured divisions, and preferred a large conscript army supported by artillery and occasionally by AFV and aircraft.
- At the start of World War II, the US Army constrained the size of the M4 Sherman so that more of these AFV could be shipped to overseas areas of operations; this deliberate preference for quantity over quality risked the lives and morale of Allied servicemen pitted against enemy AFV with superior combinations of gun power and armour (Macksey 1988, p. 130).
- During the Battle of Britain in 1940, faith in superior numbers encouraged some RAF commanders to assemble their fighter squadrons in a 'Big Wing' before engaging incoming Luftwaffe formations of bombers and fighters; full-scale adoption of this tactic would probably have been disastrous (Wood

and Dempster 1961, p. 412) and might well have lost the Battle of Britain (Overy 2001, p. 85).

- The Soviet Union, in 1941, believed in the concept of a 'mass army' and entrusted defence of its western frontier to a huge fleet of twelve thousand AFV, but only about one tenth of these were fit for armoured warfare against the majority of the AFV in the German Panzer divisions.
- Later, during the Cold War against the Soviet Union, some commentators argued that the air defence of the UK should be entrusted to large numbers of subsonic aircraft armed with short-range, infrared-guided missiles rather than relying on fewer (and more expensive) supersonic interceptors armed with long-range radar-guided missiles; fortunately it could easily be demonstrated that such subsonic aircraft would have been almost entirely ineffective (like the cheap He162 and Me163 fighters produced by the Third Reich in 1945).

It is impossible to be sure that any of the above policies were guided (consciously or unconsciously) by Lanchester's Square Law, but it is certain that, through many decades of the twentieth century, the Lanchester equations dominated the US Army's combat modelling and contributed to its selection of weapon systems (Epstein 1985)

11 Overview

11.1 Results of this Analysis

The analysis in Section 7 considered the numbers and losses of open-field battles in the ACW in terms of the numbers of troops actively engaged in each battle, rather than in terms of the numbers of troops on or near the battlefield. This analysis demonstrated that the ratio of losses sustained by the opposing armies in each battle was inversely proportional to the representative ratio of the numbers **engaged**, in accordance with Lanchester's Square Law. This analysis also suggested that there was no significant difference in the average individual effectiveness of Union and Confederate soldiers, though it is widely recognised that some elite units on both sides (such as the Union's Iron Brigade and the Texas regiments in the Confederate army) fought exceptionally well.

The supplementary analyses of battles in various other wars during the eighteenth and nineteenth centuries do not provide conclusive supporting evidence for the validity of Lanchester's Square Law, because each of these wars included too few battles, because the estimated numbers and losses in some battles were doubtful and because the outcomes of some battles were significantly affected by cavalry charges as well as by firepower. However, the outcomes of the battles in these wars are generally consistent with the Square Law, and thus tend to support the result of the analysis of battles in the ACW. The supplementary analyses also suggested that, even in scenarios where the Square Law appears to be valid, there can be very substantial differences in the individual effectiveness of the troops involved (where 'effectiveness' is an all-embracing measure including weaponry, training, leadership and tactical doctrine) and that these differences can be large enough to offset a significant inferiority of numbers.

These supplementary analyses showed that there were significant differences in the individual effectiveness of opposing soldiers:

- in 1805–7, where the effectiveness of soldiers in the French Grande Armee was about double that of soldiers in the 'ancien regime' armies of Austria, Prussia and Russia,
- in 1808–13, where the effectiveness of soldiers in British armies in the Peninsular War was about double that of the French, and
- in 1866, where the effectiveness of Prussian soldiers was about five times greater than that of the unfortunate Austrians (brave, but ill-armed and badly led).

There is ample historical evidence that, in modern warfare between developed nations, there can be similarly large differences in the individual effectiveness of fighting units (such as in Operation Barbarossa, the naval battle of Matapan and the Great Marianas Turkey Shoot) when one of the opposing forces had an appreciable advantage.

It may be concluded that, in land battles of the nineteenth century, the larger army tended to inflict more losses on the smaller (and hence to achieve victories) provided that the commander of the larger army:

- equipped his soldiers with weapon systems which matched those of the enemy,
- deployed his force effectively so that almost all of it engaged the enemy,
- did not attack field fortifications, or allow his army to be surprised, and
- devoted sufficient attention to tactics, training and morale so that his soldiers' individual effectiveness was not appreciably inferior to the enemy.

In this period, superiority of numbers was important, but victory also depended critically on many other factors, including the individual effectiveness of the soldiers involved.

This conclusion on the importance of superior numbers endorsed the well-established maxim of eighteenth and nineteenth century generals that they should assemble the largest possible number of troops before engaging in a decisive battle, rather than distributing them in irrelevant detachments. At a tactical level, it supported the twentieth-century concept of concentrating armoured fighting vehicles to rupture an enemy defensive position by overwhelming any enemy defences at the breakthrough point (as demonstrated by German Panzer corps in 1939–42). Conversely, it highlighted the futility of distributing troops in a defensive cordon which is weak everywhere and strong nowhere.

The result of the analysis of ACW battles in Section 7 emphasised that the number of troops actually engaged was more significant than the number present on or near the battlefield. It was important then, and it remains important today, for a military force to have good reconnaissance, command and control, communications, mobility and support (as discussed in Section 7) to ensure that all of the force's fighting units could be brought into action. In the Battle of Britain, for example, the RAF's early warning and command/control systems enabled it to direct its limited force of fighters to provide an effective defence of the UK, rather than wasting them on nugatory combat air patrols. There inevitably remains a (small?) risk that a national defence review might focus on simplistic totals of the number of planned fighting units (battalions, tanks, guns, warships and combat aircraft) to be deployed, without reference to their quality or to the provision of the vital non-combat elements. Ideally the results of this study will reduce that risk.

11.2 Limited Validity of Lanchester's Square Law

This Element has identified some historical scenarios in which Lanchester's Square Law was valid and many others where it was not. It therefore highlights the **limitations** of the Square Law, and should prevent it from being applied indiscriminately and inappropriately by politicians and journalists who ought to know better. Lanchester's Square Law appears to be valid **only** in combat conditions where battles were principally decided by massed firepower, where all of the opposing forces could engage an enemy and where the larger forces could exploit converging fire (i.e. in the land battles of the ACW and of the preceding century, including the Napoleonic period). There are insufficient data to support a comparable analysis of naval or air warfare; the Square Law might possibly be valid for some particular scenarios, but in naval warfare the quality of individual warships and their crews was always important.

During other historical periods and in other combat scenarios, the assumptions underlying Lanchester's Square Law model were unjustified and the model's conclusions would be dangerously misleading. In classical and medieval warfare, and in modern combat between armoured fighting vehicles and between combat aircraft, the quality of the individual fighting units was often more important than the scale of the forces involved. In any historical period, the force which had a longer-range weapon system – a 'Turkish' composite bow, a 'Pennsylvania' rifle or an 88 mm anti-tank gun – had a considerable and often a decisive advantage, irrespective of the numbers involved. It was always demoralising for an outclassed army to sustain losses without being able to hit back, and it could be disastrous for a warship to suffer disabling hits before it could close to within effective range of its own guns.

Lanchester's Square Law should be used only for those scenarios in which its assumptions are justifiable. Before using either the Square Law or the Linear Law or any hybrid variant to analyse historical battles, or to predict the outcomes of potential future battles, analysts should consider carefully the relevant combat conditions and must judge whether they tend to feature mass or individual actions. For example, battles between armoured fighting vehicles on the Ukrainian steppe might have been governed by the Square Law and those in the Normandy hedgerows by the Linear Law.

11.3 Planning Future Military Forces

A modern government must develop, within its armed forces, a range of military capabilities allowing them to undertake, if necessary, operations against well-armed enemies in several potential scenarios. In the planning process (generally part of a strategic defence review), the government must balance the future scale and the future quality of its armed forces within the constraints imposed by the threat(s) and by the available budgets. High-quality forces are expensive because their requirements include (as well as measures to sustain the essential qualities of motivation and morale):

• generous wages and conditions of service to attract satisfactory recruits,
• top-quality equipment and integrated logistic support, and
• rigorous training and education for all ranks, with realistic large-scale exercises.

The plans for procurement of new or upgraded weapon systems must recognise that improvements in their quality (such as range, lethality and reliability) can incur disproportionate increases in unit cost, as discussed in Section 2.4, and hence reductions in the numbers in the fleet which can be afforded from a limited budget. The armed forces must therefore model potential future operations in sufficient detail to identify the most cost-effective force mix for each of the military capabilities required by national defence policy. Modern combat models use powerful computers so there is no need today to use simplistic Lanchester models and they are now redundant. The enduring quality/quantity dilemmas involved in planning future military forces, and the associated allocation of resources, can generally be resolved by a blend of cost forecasting, operational analysis and military judgement (though inter-Service debates can be acrimonious). However, when political and public opinions are (inevitably) involved in major procurement projects, government policy may be influenced by lobbying and may also be distorted by popular belief in the presumed virtues of superior numbers, derived from an incomplete understanding of Lanchester's Square Law and its limitations. This belief was justified in a few historical scenarios but is rarely, if ever, justified today.

A modern government preparing its national armed forces for expeditionary asymmetric warfare in support of a friendly foreign government against terrorist insurgents, must provide its armed forces with sufficient equipment (such as helicopters, night-vision goggles and mine detectors) to enable its forces to defeat poorly armed but determined and ingenious insurgents wherever they can be brought to battle, and with sufficient intelligence information to direct its forces in effective and economical operations. The foreign government must also enlarge and motivate its own forces sufficiently to provide security for loyal citizens in the areas which its forces (nominally) control, and to provide adequate levels of prosperity, justice and public services in those areas to retain their loyalty. However, asymmetric warfare is primarily a protracted battle for hearts and minds, and it is ultimately decided by the resolution displayed by the expeditionary force, by the foreign government and by the insurgents. If the insurgents are sufficiently zealous, they can withstand higher attrition and eventually drive their opponents to despair and collapse. Asymmetric warfare has political, cultural and social (as well as military) dimensions, and in such warfare Lanchester's Laws are largely irrelevant.

When Lanchester's combat models were published in 1916, they were valid (when correctly interpreted) for a particular period of land warfare in the nineteenth century. They represented a notable advance in the application of mathematics to operational analysis and military planning. Although warfare changed dramatically in the twentieth century, Lanchester models were used for many decades to optimise the effectiveness of new weapon systems and to provide the foundations for high-level war gaming. During the past century, while Lanchester's Square Law was neither convincingly validated nor refuted, it remained possible that its inadequately understood conclusion would distort defence policies. This Element, which demonstrates the limitations of the Square Law, should allow a robust rejection of any exaggerated claims for the importance of superior numbers. Superior numbers remain advantageous in some modern combat scenarios, but they are often less important than the relative quality of the opposing forces. Hence, Lanchester's Square Law should be relegated to analyses of nineteenth century warfare, which was its proper historical context, and should not be quoted indiscriminately.

12 Conclusions

The analyses of ACW battles in Section 7, and the supplementary analyses of other wars in Sections 8 and 9, have demonstrated that the outcomes of land battles in the nineteenth century were indeed dependent on the ratio of the numbers of opposing troops engaged, in accordance with Lanchester's Square Law. However, the outcomes of these battles were also very significantly affected by several other factors (notably by the troops' equipment, training and leadership) and these factors must be considered when assessing the combat power of any military force, especially in modern times when advanced technology can tip the balance between victory and defeat. Karl von Clausewitz (1780–1831) could dismiss superiority in weapons as insignificant because, in his lifetime, all developed nations had essentially the same weapon systems, but today the effect of superior numbers can be offset, and frequently outweighed, by the effect of advanced weapon, sensor or communication systems.

Throughout the past century, when Lanchester's Square Law and Linear Law were neither conclusively validated nor refuted, these simplistic Laws remained enduringly attractive. They appeared to offer, to political leaders and to their military staffs, some easily understood guidance to solve their quality versus quantity dilemmas. This analysis has shown that Lanchester's Square Law (when correctly interpreted in terms of troops engaged) was valid in some particular historical scenarios, such as the land battles of the ACW which matched that Law's assumptions. In other scenarios, especially in modern warfare dominated by technology, Lanchester's Laws are potentially misleading, and they should not be used indiscriminately to guide defence planning or policy

Appendix 1

Open-Field Battles of the American Civil War, 1861–1865

This Appendix considers the open-field battles of the ACW which were judged to be suitable for this analysis of the effect of superior numbers. For each of these battles, Appendix 1 describes the process, following the principles discussed in Section 7, by which a representative ratio of the Union/Confederate forces effectively engaged was estimated from published data on the strengths of the opposing armies on or near the battlefield. The estimation process sometimes relied on uncertain data and on personal judgement, and some of the resulting force ratios might be amended by more rigorous analysis. However, such minor amendments for a few battles would not significantly affect the conclusions of this analysis.

In accordance with the principles discussed in Section 7, this database excludes battles affected by special circumstances such as:

- there was a significant difference in the training and experience of the opposing armies (as at Richmond, Kentucky),
- one of the opposing armies achieved a complete tactical surprise (as at Cedar Creek, Virginia),
- there were relatively few troops involved (as in the 1862 campaign in the Shenandoah Valley) and the outcomes were consequently affected by particular details of topography, etc.
- there is great uncertainty about the numbers engaged (as at Savage Station and Chantilly) or about the losses sustained (as at Pea Ridge and in the 1865 battles), and
- the battle extended over more than one day with substantial variations in the ratio of troops involved and with no credible estimates of losses sustained in different phases of the battle.

For each battle, the estimates of numbers and losses have been derived from several sources of which only the principal specific source is cited below.

First Bull Run, 21 July 1861 Both of the opposing armies had about 30,000 men on the battlefield, but only about 18,000 from each army were fully engaged (McPherson 1988, p. 344). The strength ratio of troops actively engaged varied through the day as successive Confederate and Union brigades came into action. Lacking a detailed chronology, a Union/Confederate (U/C) strength ratio of unity is probably not far wrong. Current estimates of the losses vary, but most give a U/C loss ratio which is close to Livermore's 1.37.

Wilson's Creek, 10 August 1861 The latest studies (Piston 2000 and Brookshaw 1995) of the battle suggests that the U/C ratio of troops present was 5,431/10,125 = 0.54, excluding from the Confederate total some 2,000 members of the Missouri State Guard who were unarmed and unorganised and hence could play little part in the battle. Other Confederate units, such as Brown's cavalry and the 4th and 5th regiments of Arkansas infantry, suffered negligible losses and cannot have been fully engaged. Deducting troops not engaged and a quarter of the cavalry in both armies to act as horse-holders, gives a U/C ratio of troops engaged of 5246/7545 = 0.70. This ratio probably exaggerates the Confederate strength because the surprised Confederate units came into action progressively, and because their outlying cavalry units were surprised and scattered early in the day (probably losing a considerable number of stragglers). A strength ratio of 0.8 is probably more representative and was used in this analysis. The same studies suggest that the U/C loss ratio was 1,317/1,222 = 1.08, which is close to the ratios in other histories.

Shiloh, 6 April 1862 The U/C strength ratios on 6 and 7 April were very different because the Union army received large reinforcements overnight, so this analysis has focussed on the first day of the battle, which saw the most intense fighting and most of the losses. At dawn on the 6th, the Union Army of the Tennessee had 39,830 men camped at Shiloh; during the latter part of the day it was reinforced by Ammen's brigade of the Army of the Ohio which arrived in time to participate in the battle, and by Wallace's errant division which did not. The Confederate Army of the Mississippi attacked with 43,968, giving a U/C strength ratio of 41,358/43,968 = 0.94. There is inevitably some uncertainty about which losses were incurred on which day, but the latest analysis suggest that the U/C loss ratio on the 6th was 10,720/9,968 = 1.08 (Martin 1987).

Fort Magruder, 5 May 1862 There were two engagements, concurrent but separate, fought near Williamsburg on that date; one major battle was near Fort Magruder and the other smaller battle (where neither force lost more than 1,000) was two miles farther north near Cub Creek. At Fort Magruder, the Union army had some 41,000 troops near the battlefield but most of them were not engaged. Throughout the morning, General Hooker's Union division was outnumbered by five (later six) Confederate brigades, and some of Hooker's regiments were forced to withdraw before he was reinforced by General Kearny's division in mid-afternoon. For most of the day, the U/C strength ratio at Fort Magruder was about 0.8, and the U/C loss ratio there was 2,183/1,174 = 1.86 (Sears 1992 and Martin 1992).

Seven Pines, 31 May 1862 In the first phase, four Confederate brigades (9,000) from General D. H. Hill's division attacked General Casey's Union division (6,200) in a partially fortified position. Most of Casey's division was routed and took no further part in the battle (Dwight 1895, p. 195). In the second, phase the Confederate force was reinforced by Colonel Jenkin's brigade (1,900) and defeated four fresh Union brigades from General Couch's and General Kearney's divisions; this phase involved similar numbers of troops in the opposing forces. Hence a U/C strength ratio of 0.85 is reasonably representative of the whole battle. The U/C loss ratio was 3,360/3,732 = 0.90 (Sears 1992 and Martin 1987).

Fair Oaks 31 May 1862 This battle involved four Confederate brigades from General Whiting's division against four Union brigades, three from General Sedgwick's division and one from General Couch's. The nominal U/C strength ratio was 10,700/8,700 = 1.23, but since one of the Confederate brigades arrived near the end of the battle a ratio of 1.40 is probably more representative. The Union force was supported by two batteries of artillery, but the Confederates had none. The U/C loss ratio was 468/1,270 = 0.37 (Sears 1992 and Martin 1987).

Orchard Station, 1 June 1862 Following the battle of Seven Pines, six fresh Confederate brigades attacked five fresh Union brigades but were repulsed. The overall U/C strength ratio was probably about 14,900/11,500 = 1.30, and the U/C loss ratio was 1,203/1,132 = 1.03 (Sears 1992 and Martin 1987).

Glendale, 30 June 1862 The Seven Days campaign in defence of Richmond started with a skirmish at Oak Grove on 25 June, continued with two Confederate assaults on fortified lines at Mechanicsville on the 26th and Gaines Mill on the 27th, followed by a skirmish at Savage Station on the 29th. The losses incurred by both armies in these successive engagements must be taken into account when estimating the numbers engaged in later battles. At Glendale, the Confederate divisions of Generals Longstreet and A. P. Hill (together about 18,000 men) attacked elements of several Union divisions deployed around the Glendale crossroads. About 37,000 Union troops were engaged by the end of the day but the nominal U/C strength ratio of 2.06 exaggerates the Union advantage. General McCall's Union division (7,500) was defeated and largely dispersed before the other Union forces came into action, and some Union reinforcements (some 11,700) only arrived towards the end of the day. Assuming for this analysis that McCall fought only in the first half of the battle and the reinforcements only in the second half, the effective U/C strength ratio was approximated as (37,000 − 9,600)/18,000 = 1.52. The U/C loss ratio was 2,853/3,300 = 0.85 (Dowdey 1964 and Sears 1992)).

Malvern Hill, 1 July 1862 There were about 80,000 troops in each of the opposing armies on this battlefield but fewer than half were actively engaged. Probably about 30,000 Confederate infantry attacked a similar number of Union infantry, giving a U/C strength ratio of unity (Sears 1992). However this ratio should ideally be increased because the Confederate attacks were uncoordinated and each successive brigade-level attack was subjected to converging fire from superior numbers, directly ahead of the attackers and on both flanks. The U/C loss ratio was 3,007/5,250 = 0.53. This loss ratio was reduced by the unusually large array of field and heavy artillery which supported the Union infantry, and which was assessed to have inflicted about half of the Confederate losses (Naisawand 1960, p. 135).

Cedar Mountain, 9 August 1862 At the start of this battle, four Union brigades (8,000) attacked four Confederate brigades (7,400) and initially had some success. During the battle, the Confederate force was reinforced by General A. P. Hill's division but only three of his brigades were actively engaged. By the end of the battle, the U/C ratio of troops engaged was 8,800/13,100 = 0.67, but, since Hill's brigades arrived part way through the battle, a U/C ratio of troops engaged of 8,800/10,700 = 0.77 is probably more representative. There were about 7,000 more Confederate troops on the battlefield but they suffered negligible losses and cannot have been closely engaged. Histories of the battle give the U/C loss ratio as 2,275/1,355 = 1.68 (Henderson 1897 and Stackpole 1993).

Groveton, 28 August 1862 This battle began with an engagement between the Union 2nd Wisconsin regiment and the Confederate Stonewall brigade, and escalated as both commanders brought additional units into action. By nightfall, six Union regiments and four Confederate brigades (and part of another which arrived very late in the battle) had been actively engaged. The U/C ratio of strength engaged fluctuated as successive reinforcements arrived but a value of 0.7 is probably representative. Estimates of the U/C loss ratio vary between unity and 0.92 so this analysis has used 0.96 (Henderson 1897 and Stackpole 1993).

Turner's Gap, 14 September 1862 On this day, there was a skirmish at Crampton's Gap (where the losses were too small to be included in this analysis) and a battle on both sides of Turner's Gap, where the turnpike road from Frederick to Boonsboro crosses South Mountain. This battle involved several discrete engagements (extending from Fox's Gap in the south to the Zittlestown Road in the north) with various strength ratios and loss ratios, but the overall U/C strength ratio of troops engaged was about 2. However some units on both sides were only lightly engaged, and some of the engagement started at brigade level with U/C ratios of about unity. Because of the diseconomies of scale discussed in Section 7.4, an average U/C ratio of strength engaged of 1.6 is probably more representative. Most of the estimated U/C loss ratios lie between 0.67 and 0.80 so this analysis uses 0.75; this ratio is inflated by the advantageous position of the Confederates on higher ground in some of the engagements (Priest 1992 and Carman 2010).

Antietam, 17 September 1862 This battle featured a succession of Union corps-level attacks on the northern, central and finally the southern parts of the Confederate army's position. The battle continued all day but most units were in action for only a few hours. Accordingly, this analysis gave equal weight to all of the opposing units engaged, including the three brigades of General A. P. Hill's division which arrived and went into action near the end of the day. Livermore's original estimates of the U/C strength ratio on the battlefield took no account of the large-scale straggling by Confederate troops who were exhausted by many weeks of intensive campaigning and/or had moral objections to invading Union territory. Modern analyses, taking account of Confederate straggling and also of Union troops who were present but were retained in reserve, have suggested a U/C ratio of troops engaged of 56,000/40,000 = 1.40. Many Confederate units either submitted incomplete reports of their losses (or no reports at all) or merged their losses in this battle with other losses in the Maryland campaign. Most modern histories set the Confederate losses at Antietam at 10,318; using that number in this analysis gives a U/C loss ratio of 12,410/10,318 = 1.2 (Murfin 1965 and Priest 1989).

Perryville, 6 October 1862 At Perryville, the Union army had many more troops on the battlefield but fewer than half of them were actively engaged. All of General Crittenden's corps and five of General Gilbert's nine brigades incurred only trivial losses, as did General Wheeler's Confederate cavalry. Omitting these units gave for this analysis a U/C ratio of troops engaged of 21,500/14,800 = 1.45. The U/C loss ratio was 4,211/3,396 = 1.24 (Brown 2000).

Prairie Grove, 7 December 1862 This was a meeting engagement in which a Confederate army of 11,500 moved between two Union forces (General Herron's 6,000 and General Blunt's 7,000) hoping to defeat them in succession. The Confederates attacked Herron first, but Blunt marched to the sound of guns and joined the battle in progress. The opposing armies were depleted by forced marches in bad weather, so the U/C strength ratio is uncertain, but was probably around 10,000/9,000 = 1.11. The U/C loss ratio was 1,251/1,317 = 0.95 (Christ 2010).

Fredericksburg, Prospect Hill, 13 December 1862 At the northern end of the Fredericksburg battlefield, the Union army sustained heavy losses attacking a strong Confederate position incorporating a sunken road used as a trench. The southern part of the Confederate position near Prospect Hill was not fortified, and in that area the Union divisions of Generals Meade, Gibbon and Birney fought against the Confederate divisions of Generals Early and A. P. Hill. In this engagement, the U/C strength ratio was $16,600/22,187 = 0.75$ and the loss ratio was $4,075/3,072 = 1.33$ (Stackpole 1957).

Stone's River, 31 December 1862 In the first phase of this battle, on 31 December, the Confederates made a largely successful surprise attack on the Union right wing and drove it a couple of miles rearward. Later that day, successive Confederate attacks failed to dislodge the Union army from a strong position in the Round Forest of cedars. Two days later, on 2 January 1863, General Breckenridge's Confederate division attacked the Union left; that attack was initially successful but was then defeated with the help of a massed battery of 45 Union guns. The U/C strength ratio was $47,000/38,000 = 1.24$. The U/C loss ratio over all three days was $13,249/11,739 = 1.13$; this ratio was increased by the effects of the Confederate surprise on the 31st, and reduced by the heavy losses sustained by Breckenridge on 2 January (Cozzens 1991 and Horn 1941).

Chancellorsville, Fairview Salient, 3 May 1863 The fighting in the concurrent engagements around Chancellorsville and Fredricksburg extended over four days, 1 to 4 May. It consisted of a series of seven discrete engagements separated in time and space and involving parts of the opposing armies. The U/C ratio of troops present was $135000/59000 = 2.3$, but the Union I corps and most of the V corps were only lightly engaged and most of the Union cavalry was detached on a raid, Accordingly the U/C ratio of troops engaged through the four days of battle was $102,000/59,000 = 1.73$. The overall U/C loss ratio covering all engagements was reported to be $17,287/12,821 = 1.35$, but this ratio is suspect because several Confederate units reported no soldiers missing, and the ratio is atypically inflated by the losses inflicted by the flank attack on the Union XI corps on the evening of 2 May. It is generally impractical to estimate the strength and loss ratios for each of the individual engagements, but fortunately such estimates have been derived (Sears 1996) for the largest engagement which was fought on 3 May by three Union corps defending the Fairview salient against most of the Confederate army. In that engagement, the U/C strength ratio was about unity, and the U/C loss ratio was $8,623/8,962 = 0.96$. In this engagement, the Union forces had some advantage from improvised field fortifications, but were vulnerable to Confederate artillery at Hazel Grove, so the strength and loss ratios are probably representative.

Champion Hill, 16 May 1863 This was the only large-scale open-field battle in the Vicksburg campaign. Most accounts agree with Livermore's estimates of the numbers of troops present, yielding a U/C strength ratio of troops present of 29,373/20,000 = 1.45. However several units in both armies failed to participate, and the U/C ratio of troops actually engaged was 20,000/13,000 = 1.54. The U/C loss ratio was 2,441/3,851 = 0.63 (Arnold 1997).

Gettysburg, North and West, 1 July 1863 In the meeting engagement on 1 July, four Confederate divisions attacked and defeated a Union force of two infantry corps and a cavalry division. Some parts of these opposing formations were absent that day and other parts were not actively engaged. The U/C strength ratio of troops engaged that day was 19,270/24,854 = 0.78 and the U/C loss ratio was 1.4 (Sears 2003 and Pfanz 2001).

Gettysburg, Peach Orchard, Wheatfield and Little Round Top, 2 July 1863 During the afternoon of 2nd July the Union III corps advanced into a vulnerable salient with its apex at the Peach Orchard, where it was attacked by eleven Confederate brigades. As the Confederate echeloned attack developed, Union reinforcements from the II and V corps were deployed to resist the attack. By evening the U/C ratio of troops involved was about 28,000/18,500 = 1.51. However the Union reinforcements arrived progressively, so that in the early engagements (at Houck Ridge, Little Round Top and The Wheatfield) the Confederate forces had superior numbers. In the later engagements the Union forces had superior numbers, and it is reasonable to assume for this analysis that a U/C strength ratio of unity was reasonably representative. The U/C loss ratio for that afternoon, in the Peach Orchard salient, was 9,000/6,000 = 1.5 (Adkin 2008 and Pfanz 1987).

Chickamauga, 19 to 20 September 1863 During this two-day battle, both armies received some reinforcements, and on the first day there was a meeting engagement in which additional divisions from each army came into action successively. The U/C strength ratio must have fluctuated through the two days but was probably never very far from the overall value of 57,000/66,300 = 0.86. The U/C loss ratio was 16,129/17,804 = 0.91; this ratio was reduced by the breastworks constructed by Union troops to defend their positions in the later phases of the battle, and contrariwise was increased by the confusion in Union command and control which allowed a Confederate breakthrough on the second day (Tucker 1984).

Mansfield, 8 April 1864 A small Confederate army of 9,000 faced 20,000 Union troops advancing in column. The Confederates attacked and defeated the leading two Union contingents but were repulsed by the third which had incorporated some of the Union troops defeated earlier. It is unclear how many of those Union troops rallied to fight again, and how many Confederate troops straggled during their army's advance. The average U/C ratio of troops engaged in the three phases of the battle was probably about 0.6. The U/C loss ratio was 2,232/1,000 = 2.23 (Johnson 1995).

Pleasant Hill, 9 April 1864 During the night after the battle of Mansfield, both armies received reinforcements, giving a U/C strength ratio of 12,100/12,500 = 0.97, and the Union army established itself in a chosen defensive position. The Confederates made a flank march and successfully attacked the left end of the Union line but were ultimately defeated by veteran Union reserves. The U/C loss ratio was 1,369/1,626 = 0.84.

Drewry's Bluff, 16 May 1864 A Confederate attack was partially successful but the plan for a concentric envelopment of the Union army miscarried when a Confederate division commander had a nervous breakdown and failed to advance. The battle ended with a voluntary Union withdrawal. The U/C strength ratio was 15,800/18,025 = 0.88 and the loss ratio was 4,160/2,506 = 1.66 (Williams 1995).

Piedmont, 5 June 1864 A small Confederate army tried to stop a Union advance through the Shenandoah Valley. The outnumbered Confederate army had some field fortifications, but its troops had been hastily and inadequately deployed. The U/C strength ratio was 12,000/5,600 = 2.14, but the larger force would have been unable to bring all its troops into effective action simultaneously (as discussed in Section 7.4), so this analysis assumed that a U/C ratio of strength engaged 1.75 was probably more representative. The loss ratio was 875/1,600 = 0.55 (Kennedy 1990).

Monocacy, 9 July 1864 During the last Confederate invasion of Union territory, a Union army accepted battle against superior numbers in order to delay the Confederate advance on Washington, DC. The Union army had a good defensive position guarding all of the bridges across the Monocacy River, but a Confederate division crossed by a ford beyond the Union left and after hard fighting dislocated the Union line. Other Confederate divisions were then able to cross the river and join the battle. The U/C strength ratio of troops present was about 5,800/15,000 but only two thirds of the Confederate army engaged and only one third (General Gordon's infantry division and a cavalry brigade) did most of the fighting. A time-averaged U/C ratio of troops engaged of 5,800/(5,000 + 5,000/2) = 0.77 is probable representative. The U/C loss ratio was 1,300/800 = 1.63. There is considerable variation in the battle data cited in different histories.

Fisher's Hill, 22 September 1842 The Confederates occupied a strong position but only fortified part of it. A Union corps successfully outflanked the Confederate left and advanced into the rear of the Confederate army while the rest of the Union army made a direct attack. Outnumbered and outflanked, the Confederate army disintegrated and fled. The U/C ratio of strength engaged is given in most histories as $29,400/9,500 = 3.09$, but since the Union VI and XIX corps suffered losses of around 1.5 per cent it can be inferred that some units in these two corps were not actively engaged. For this analysis, it was assumed that, because of the diseconomies of scale discussed in Section 7.4, a U/C ratio of strength engaged of 2.38 would be more representative. This estimate is uncertain but it is probably nearer the true ratio than 3.09. The U/C loss ratio was $528/1,235 = 0.43$ (Osborne 1992).

Data Sources for Appendix 1

Adkin, M. (2008) *The Gettysburg Companion*, London: Aurum Press.

Arnold, J. (1997) *Grant wins the War*, New York: Wiley and Co.

Brookshaw, W. (1995) *Bloody Hill*, London: Brasseys.

Brown, K. (2000) *The Civil War in Kentucky*, Mason City, IA: Savas Publishing.

Carman, E. (2010) *The Maryland Campaign*, Volume 1, El Dorado Hills, CA: Saras Beattie.

Christ, M. (2010) *Civil War in Arkansas 1863*, Norman: University of Oklahoma Press.

Cozzens, P. (1991) *No Better Place to Die*, Chicago: University of Illinois Press.

Dowdey, C. (1964) *The Seven Days: Emergence of Robert E. Lee*, New York: Fairfax Press.

Dwight, T. (1895) *Campaigns in Virginia 1861–62*, New York: Houghton Mifflin and Co.

Henderson, G (1897) *Stonewall Jackson*, New York: Longman Green and Co.

Horn, S. (1941) *The Army of Tennessee*, Indianapolis: Bobbs Merrill.

Johnson, L. (1995) *Red River Campaign*, Kent, OH: Kent State University Press.

Kennedy, F. (1990) *The Civil War Battlefield Guide*, Boston: Houghton Mifflin.

Martin, D. (1987) *The Shiloh Campaign*, Pittsburg, PA: Combined Press.

Martin, D. (1992) *The Peninsular Campaign*, Pittsburg, PA: Combined Press.

Murfin, J. (1965) *The Gleam of Bayonets*, Baton Rouge: Louisiana State University Press.

Naisawand, L. (1960) *Grape and Canister*, Washington, DC: Zenger Publishing.

Osborne, C. (1992) *Jubal*, Baton Rouge: Louisiana State University Press.

Pfanz, H. (2001) *Gettysburg: The First Day*, Chapel Hill: University of North Carolina Press.

Pfanz, H. (1987) *Gettysburg: The Second Day*, Chapel Hill: University of North Carolina Press.

Piston, W. (2000) *Wilson's Creek*, Chapel Hill: University of North Carolina Press.

Priest, J. (1989) *Antietam: The Soldiers' Battle*, Oxford: Oxford University Press.

Priest, J. (1992) *Before Antietam*, Oxford: Oxford University Press.

Sears, S. (1992) *To the Gates of Richmond*, New York: Ticknor and Fields.

Sears, S. (1996) *Chancellorsville*, New York: Houghton Mifflin.

Sears, S. (2003) *Gettysburg*, New York: Houghton Mifflin.

Stackpole, E. (1957) *The Fredricksburg Campaign*, Pennsylvania: Telegraph Press.

Stackpole E. (1993) *From Cedar Mountain to Antietam*, Pennsylvania: Stackpole Books.

Tucker, G. (1984) *Chickamauga*, Ohio: Morningside House.

Williams, T (1995) *P. G. T. Beauregard*, Baton Rouge: Louisiana State University Press.

Appendix 2
The Seven Years War, 1756–1763

There were thirteen major battles in the Seven Years War, of which eight were fought between the Prussians and the Austrians. One of these (Breslau) was an assault on a Prussian entrenched camp and is omitted from the analysis. For the remaining seven battles, there is considerable variation in the historical estimates of the numbers of troops present in the opposing armies, and the battle narratives are often too ambiguous to assess with confidence the (varying) ratio of troops engaged. For each battle, a representative ratio of troops engaged has been estimated from the best available evidence, as discussed in the following battle summaries. Similarly, the data on the losses from the defeated army do not distinguish between the losses incurred during the battle and those incurred during a disorderly retreat (in the aftermath of Torgau, for example, the Erzherzog Karl regiment was cut off from the rest of the Austrian army and surrendered en masse). It would be unrealistic, for the three battles in which the defeated Austrians lost a relatively large number of prisoners/missing, to assume either that all of these losses were incurred during the battle or that all were incurred during the retreat. In this analysis, it is assumed that half of such losses were incurred during the retreat and this assumption has a significant effect on the estimated loss ratios in some battles.

Lobositz, 1 October 1756 The Prussian/Austrian ratio of troops present was $29,000/34,500 = 0.84$ but it appears that part of the Austrian left wing was not engaged, so this analysis estimated the ratio of troops engaged as unity. The Prussian/Austrian loss ratio was $2,906/2,873 = 1.01$. More than a third of the Prussian army was cavalry, but the victory was won by the firepower of the Prussian infantry.

Prague, 6 May 1757 Both of the opposing armies had about 65,000 troops. The Prussians tried to outflank the Austrians who redeployed on a new defensive line. It is not clear how many troops were involved in the successive engagements of this manoeuvre battle, so this analysis used a Prussian/Austrian ratio of troops engaged of unity. The sources agree that the Prussians lost 14300 men and the Austrians lost 13400 including 4500 prisoners. Accordingly this analysis estimated the Prussian/Austrian loss ratio during the battle at $14,300/(13,400 - 4,500/2) = 1.28$.

Kolin, 18 June 1757 The Prussians launched a frontal attack on a larger Austrian army, which had successfully redeployed to block the Prussian outflanking manoeuvre. The Prussian/Austrian ratio of troops engaged was probably close to $34,000/53,000 = 0.64$, the same as ratio of troops present. The Prussian/Austrian loss ratio was $13,800/9,000 = 1.53$.

Leuthen, 5 December 1757 The strength of the Prussian army was estimated by various sources in the range $33,000 – 40,000$; most estimates were near the lower end, so this analysis used 35,000. Similarly the strength of the Austrian army was estimated in the range $53,000 – 80,000$, so this analysis used 66,000. King Frederick the Great secretly marched the Prussian army around the Austrian left flank and attacked with numerical superiority at the point of impact. The Austrian left wing consisted largely of fragile Baden and Wurttemberg battalions which were routed early in the battle. The Prussians then defeated the remainder of the Austrian army in a series of engagements in which the ratio of troops engaged was probably close to unity. The Prussians lost 6,300 men. Estimates of the Austrian losses vary between 7,000 and 10,000 killed and wounded plus between 12,000 and 22,000 prisoners/missing, so this analysis assessed the Austrian battle losses at an intermediate value of 8,500 killed and wounded plus half of an intermediate value of 17,000 prisoners/missing, giving $8,500 + 17,000/2 = 17,000$. Hence the Prussian/Austrian loss ratio was $6,300/17,000 = 0.37$.

Hochkirch, 11 August 1758 Some 80,000 Austrians were present but it was estimated that only 60,000 engaged. Most sources agree that the strength of the Prussian army was 31,000, yielding a Prussian/Austrian strength ratio of 0.52. There is a reasonable consensus that the Prussian/Austrian loss ratio was $9,100/7,600 = 1.20$.

Leignitz, 15 October 1760 There were about 30,000 Prussians and 90,000 Austrians on or near the battlefield but only part (14,000) of the Prussian army and Loudon's Austrian corps (24,000) were actually engaged in the battle. Loudon's corps was marching in column when it blundered into the Prussian line of battle, and parts of this corps made a succession of attacks. At any time, the ratio of troops in action was probably about unity. The Prussians lost 3,400 men and the Austrians lost 8,500 including 4000 prisoners, giving an estimated loss ratio during the battle of $3,400/(8,500 – 4,000/2) = 0.52$.

Torgau, 3 November 1760 Frederick the Great divided the Prussian army of 48,500 into four columns and led three of them (30,500) around the western flank of the Austrian army of 53,000, part of which redeployed to oppose Frederick's

Table 3 Battle data from the Seven Years War

Battle	Prussian strength	Austrian strength	Prussian loss	Austrian loss	Log P/A strength engaged	Log P/A loss in battle	Log A/P effectiveness
Lobositz	29,000	34,500	2,906	2,873	0	+0.01	+0.01
Prague	65,000	65,000	14,300	11,150	0	+0.11	+0.11
Kolin	34,000	53,000	13,800	9,000	−0.19	+0.19	0
Leuthen	35,000	66,000	6,300	25,500	0	−0.43	
Hochkirch	31,000	60,000	9,100	7,600	−0.29	+0.08	−0.21
Leignitz	14,000	24,000	3,400	8,500	0	−0.28	−0.28
Torgau	48,500	53,000	16,700	15,700	−0.13	+0.14	+0.01
Average of 6							−0.06

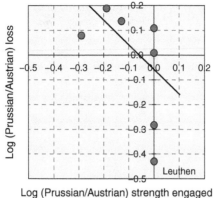

Log (Prussian/Austrian) strength engaged

Figure 3 Variation of the ratio of Austrian/Prussian losses with ratio of Prussian/Austrian strengths engaged

columns. The flank march by these columns was delayed and disrupted, and they attacked in small detachments as they arrived (the first Prussian attack involved only 9,000 troops against superior numbers of Austrians). The fourth column (18,000), commanded by Ziethen, did not come into action until late in the battle. The Prussian/Austrian ratio of troops present was 0.92 but the ratio of troops engaged during most of the battle must have been significantly smaller; this analysis noted that Ziethen's corps were in action for about half of the battle and estimated the ratio of troops engaged at $(30,500 + 18,000/2)/53,000 = 0.75$. The Prussians lost 16,700 men (and Frederick tried to conceal that large number) while the Austrians lost 8,700 killed and wounded and 7,000 prisoners. This analysis estimated the Prussian/Austrian loss ratio during the battle at $16,700/(8,700 + 7,000/2) = 1.37$ (see Table 3 and Figure 3).

Synopsis Apart from the outlier Leuthen, which was regarded as an exceptional triumph at the time and in all subsequent military histories, these battle data are consistent with Lanchester's Square Law. The Austrian/Prussian ratio of individual effectiveness was 1.08 when the Prussians attacked and 0.57 when the Austrians attacked. The difference probably arose from the greater impact of artillery fire on attacking infantry. The estimated ratios of strength engaged and of losses in battle could be reconsidered if additional evidence became available, but the trend of the data is evident.

Data Sources for Appendix 2

Calvert, M. (1978) *A Dictionary of Battles 1715–1815*, London: New English Library.

Duffy, C. (1974) *The Army of Frederick the Great*, London: Purnell Book Services.

Duffy, C. (1986) *Frederick the Great: A military life*. London: Routledge and Paul.

Millar, S. (2001) *Kolin 1757*, Oxford: Osprey.

Millar, S. (2002) *Rossbach and Leuthen 1757*, Oxford: Osprey.

Szabo, F. (2008) *The Seven Years War in Europe 1756–63*, Harlow: Pearson Education.

Appendix 3

The Grande Armee Rampant, 1805–1807

This analysis of the Grande Armee's campaigns against the Prussians and the Russians (with some Austrians at Austerlitz) omits sieges and capitulations where the losses of the defeated armies were inflated by large numbers of prisoners. It also omits minor clashes where the outcomes were distorted by particular circumstances. There are inevitably some variations in the estimates of numbers and losses provided by different historians.

Hollabrunn, 16 November 1805 In this battle, a Russian rear-guard (8,000) withstood the attack of a larger French force (30,000) for several hours, but only a third of the French force was actively engaged. The most detailed accounts of the battle suggest that the French/Russian ratios of numbers engaged and of losses were about 1.25 and 0.40 respectively.

Austerlitz, 2 December 1805 The larger Allied army clumsily attempted to outflank the French right wing but was disrupted by a French counter-attack in the centre. This manoeuvre isolated part of the Allied left wing, which was unable to escape across the semi-frozen lakes and marshes behind it and surrendered in large numbers. The French/Allied ratio of troops present was $73,000/83,500 = 0.87$. In the French army, 14,000 were not actively engaged; in the Allied army, 12 Russian battalions (6,000) were not actively engaged and the 4,500 Cossacks present had negligible capability on a battlefield. Accordingly, the French/Allied ratio of the total numbers engaged was about $59,000/73,000 = 0.81$, which in this analysis was assumed to be representative of the various ratios in multiple separate engagements. In the aftermath of the battle, some contingents of the Allied left wing were encircled and surrendered to the victorious French. The French lost 10,200 men, and the Allies lost 15,700 killed and wounded as well as 11,800 prisoners/missing. It was assumed that half of the Allied prisoners/missing were lost during the battle, so the ratio of battle losses was $5,500/(15,700 + 11,800/2) = 0.47$.

Jena, 14 October 1806 This battle was a meeting engagement in which an ever-increasing number of French troops attacked a Prussian and Saxon flank guard, screening the retreat of the main Prussian army towards Auerstadt. There were 96,000 French troops present in or near the battlefield against 53,000 Prussians and Saxons, but only 54,000 French troops were engaged. Initially, the various contingents of Prussians and Saxons were dispersed, and were defeated and put out of action successively by superior numbers of French troops. The French/Allied ratios of troops engaged in the successive phases of the battle varied from 1.5 up to 3, and a ratio of 2 is probably representative. The French lost about 5,500 men, and the Allied force lost 11,000 killed and wounded and 15,000 prisoners/missing. It is unclear how many of the prisoners/missing were lost during the sustained pursuit of the routed army by French cavalry, but this analysis assumed that half were captured during the battle and thus the French/Allied loss ratio was 5,500/(11,000 + 15,000/2) = 0.30.

Auerstadt, 14 October 1806 The isolated French III corps intercepted the main Prussian army retreating towards Magdeburg. The Prussian army's deployment was confused, and its attacks were poorly coordinated. Various sources estimate the strength of the French III corps between 26,000 and 29,000, and the strength of the Prussian army between 50,000 and 63,000. Taking intermediate values the French/Prussian ratio of troops present was assumed to be 27,500/56,500 = 0.49. However the King of Prussia retained 14 battalions (10,000) in reserve, and most of the Prussian artillery park (4,900) did not reach the battlefield. The French/Prussian ratio of troops engaged was therefore 27,500/42,500 = 0.65. The French lost 7,000 and the Prussians lost 10,000 killed and wounded and 3,000 prisoners. The French were too exhausted to pursue so this analysis assumed that all prisoners were taken during the battle; hence the French/Allied ratio of battle losses was 7,000/13,000 = 0.54.

Pultusk, 26 December 1806 In this battle, Marshal Lannes' French corps (19,000), reinforced later in the day by a division (7,000) from Marshal Davout's corps, attacked a Russian force of 42,000. The French/Russian strength ratio appears to have risen from 19,000/42,000 = 0.45 to 26,000/42,000 = 0.62 as French reinforcements arrived, so an intermediate ratio of 0.53 is probably representative. Different histories cite various numbers of losses but the French/Russian loss ratio was probably 7,000/5,000 = 1.4.

Eylau, 8 February 1807 At the start of the battle the French/Russian strength ratio was 45,000/67,000 = 0.67 but the progressive arrival of Marshal Davout's French corps with 15,000 more troops made the armies' strengths nearly equal. Towards the end of the battle, General Lestocq's Prussian contingent of 7,000 reinforced the Russian left wing. Part of Marshal Ney's French corps arrived on the battlefield too late to influence the outcome. The closing French/Allied strength ratio of 60,000/74,000 = 0.82 is probably representative of this battle. The French and Russian commanders reported vastly different estimates of the

Table 4 Battle data from the Napoleonic Wars 1805–7

Battle	French strength	Allied strength	French loss	Allied loss	Log F/A Strength engaged	Log F/A Loss in battle	Log A/F effectiveness
Hollabrunn	30,000	8,000	1,200	3,000	+0.10	−0.40	−0.30
Austerlitz	73,000	83,500	10,200	27,500	−0.09	−0.33	−0.42
Jena	96,000	53,000	5,500	26,000	+0.30	−0.52	−0.22
Auerstadt	27,500	56,500	7,000	13,000	−0.19	−0.27	−0.46
Pultusk	26,000	42,000	7,000	5,000	−0.27	+0.15	−0.12
Eylau	60,000	74,000	20,000	20,000	−0.09	0	−0.09
Friedland	80,000	60,000	10,000	20,000	0	−0.30	−0.30
Average of 7							−0.27

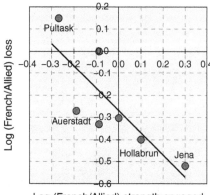

Figure 4 Variation of the ratio of French/Allied losses with the ratio of French/
Allied strengths engaged

losses suffered by the opposing armies, but most histories accept that both armies suffered similar losses, so for this analysis it was assumed that the loss ratio was 1.0.

Friedland, 14 June 1807 This battle was fought in two phases, separated by an exhausted pause. In the early morning, Marshal Lannes' outnumbered French corps resisted attacks by the part of the Russian army which had crossed the River Alle and deployed around the town of Friedland. During the early skirmishing, the strength ratio fluctuated as more Russians crossed the river and as Lannes received reinforcements. By 0800 h, when the Russians launched a general attack, the French/Russian strength ratio was 20,000/40,000 = 0.5, but by 1000 hours the ratio had grown to 40,000/45,000 = 0.89. During the afternoon, Emperor Napoleon assembled his forces and the Russians waited for darkness in the hope that they could then withdraw undetected to the safer east bank of the Alle. After 1700 h, Napoleon engaged about 65,000 of the 80,000 French troops present against the 60,000 Russians now in and around Friedland on the west bank of the Alle, giving a French/Russian strength ratio of 1.08 in this phase. Since this later phase involved the heaviest fighting, a strength ratio of 1.0 is probably representative of the battle as a whole. The French/Russian loss ratio during the battle was probably 10,000/20,000 = 0.5, but the Russians also lost many drowned trying to retreat across the Alle (see Table 4).

Synopsis Figure 4 shows that data from the 1805–7 battles broadly follows the trend predicted by Lanchester's Square Law. The outcomes are scattered by inept leadership on one side or the other, or by the impact of untimely weather (such as the snowstorm which disrupted a major French attack at Eylau).

Data Sources for Appendix 3

Calvert, M. (1978) *A Dictionary of Battles 1715–1815*, London: New English Library.

Chandler, D. (1966) *The Campaigns of Napoleon*, New York: Macmillan Publishing.

Chandler, D. (1993) *Jena 1806*, Oxford: Osprey Publishing.

Esposito, V. (1999) *A Military History and Atlas of the Napoleonic Wars*, London: Greenhill Books.

Goetz, R. (2005) 1805 *Austerlitz*, London: Greenhill Books.

Petre, E. (1972) *Naploeon's Conquest of Prussia*, London: Arms and Armour.

Petre, E. (1989) *Napoleon's Campaign in Poland 1806–07*, London: Greenhill Books.

Rothenberg, G. (1997) *The Art of Warfare in the Age of Napoleon*: Kent, Spellmount.

Smith, D. (1998) *Napoleonic Wars Data Book*, London: Greenhill Books.

Summerville, C. (2006) *Napoleon's Polish Gamble*, Yorkshire: Pen and Sword.

Appendix 4
Peninsular War, 1808–1813

This Appendix considers those Peninsular War battles in which the majority of Allied troops were British, and also Albuera where the British contingent was 40 per cent of the Allied army but sustained most of the losses.

Vimiero, 21 August 1808 There were nearly 19,000 British and Portugese troops on or near the battlefield opposed to 13,000 French, but some of the Allied troops were not engaged. The overall French/Allied ratio of troops engaged was 13,056/10,475 = 1.23. However, because the victorious Allied troops participated in more than one engagement whereas the defeated French did not, the actual ratios of troops engaged in the five successive engagements (attacks by French brigades of Generals Charlot and Thomares, St.Clair, Maransin, Solignac and Brennier) varied considerably, from 0.44 to 1.2. The average French/British ratio of troops engaged was 0.82, which is approximately representative of the conditions of combat and will be used in this analysis. The total French/British loss ratio was 1,800/720 = 2.50.

Corunna, 16 January 1809 The battle of Corunna was fought after the British army had retreated through the mountains of Galicia in mid-winter, pursued by a larger French army. The forced marches in atrocious weather had depleted the effective strength of both armies, so the numbers deployed on the battlefield must be inferred from muster returns compiled some weeks before and some weeks after the battle. Most sources agree that there were some 15,000 British troops (almost all infantry) on the battlefield, but estimates of the strength of the French army vary from 16,000 to 24,000 (both French totals including about 4,000 cavalry whose effectiveness was largely negated by unfavourable terrain). Adopting an intermediate French strength of 20,000, which is consistent with the French muster roll two weeks later, the histories of the battle suggest that about half of the French infantry and a third of the cavalry were actively engaged, with a total of 9,300. Only thirteen of the thirty British battalions present were engaged; these included two particularly strong Guards battalions so the French/Allied ratio of troops engaged was 9,300/7,000 = 1.33. It is similarly difficult to estimate the losses of the opposing armies because many units did not distinguish between losses during the preceding forced marches and losses in the battle itself. The French/Allied ratio of battle losses was probably about 1,400/800 = 1.75

Talavera, 28 July 1809 In this battle, a French army attacked a larger Allied army of British and Spanish forces (55,000), but the French concentrated their attacks on the left of the Allied line of battle where the British were deployed). The French army had some 46,000 men, but 14,700 of these were held in reserve or faced the Spanish army without coming into action. The British army had some 19,800 men (after the losses incurred on the previous day) and was assisted by some 3,000 Spaniards on the left wing of their army. The French/Allied ratio of troops engaged was therefore 31,300/22,809 = 1.37. The French/Allied loss ratio was 6,868/4,731 = 1.45.

Bussaco, 27 September 1810 This was an anomalous battle in which only parts of the opposing armies were engaged. The French attacked up a steep rough hillside without artillery support, and accordingly suffered much heavier losses than the defending British and Portugese. The French/Allied ratio of troops engaged was 26,000/14,000 = 1.85 and the French/Allied loss ratio was 4,498/1,252 = 3.59. Several of the rearward battalions in the French attacking columns, including six battalions (3,500) in Margognet's brigade, advanced far enough to take losses from the British artillery but not far enough to fire their own muskets; hence at least 3,500 should be subtracted from the number of French troops engaged giving a more-realistic value of 22,500/14,000 = 1.61.

Barrosa, 5 March 1811 An Allied force of 5,200 fought with a French force of 7,350 of which 550 grenadiers were little engaged. The French/Allied strength ratio of troops engaged was 6,800/5,200 = 1.31 and the loss ratio was 2,062/1,238 = 1.66.

Fuentes d'Onoro, 5 May 1811 This battle was preceded by a skirmish for the possession of the village of Fuentes d'Onoro two days earlier. On 5 May, a part of the French army outflanked the Allied right flank and drove it back three miles, but the French advance was ultimately blocked by redeployed Allied troops; the concurrent French attacks on the village were costly failures. Only about half of each army was actively engaged. The French/Allied strength ratio of troops engaged was 20,573/19,233 = 1.07 and the loss ratio on the 5th was 2,192/1,500 = 1.46.

Albuera, 16 May 1811 A French army tried to outflank a larger Allied army of British, Portugese and Spanish troops, but was blocked and counter-attacked by Allied troops redeploying to their right flank. Most of the French and about two thirds of the Allied armies were actively engaged, giving a French/Allied strength ratio of 22,000/25,340 = 0.87. The official French losses were given as 5,396, but later histories estimate the true total to have been between 7,000

Table 5 Battle data from the Peninsular War 1808–13

Battle	French strength present	Allied strength present	French loss	Allied loss	Log F/A Strength engaged	Log F/A Loss in battle	Log A/F effectiveness
Vimiero	13,000	19,000	1,800	720	−0.09	+0.40	+0.31
Corunna	20,000	15,000	1,400	800	+0.12	+0.24	+0.36
Talavera	46,000	55,000	6,868	4,731	+0.14	+0.16	+0.30
Bussaco	26,000	14,000	4,498	1,252	+0.21	+0.55	
Barrosa	7,350	5,200	2,062	1,238	+0.12	+0.22	+0.34
Fuentes d'O	48,452	37,504	2,192	1,500	+0.03	+0.16	+0.19
Albuera	24,260	35,284	7,800	5,800	−0.06	+0.20	+0.14
Salamance	49,000	52,000	14,000	4,762	0	+0.43	+0.43
Vitoria	57,000	75,000	8,008	5,158	+0.05	+0.22	+0.27
Average of 8							+0.29

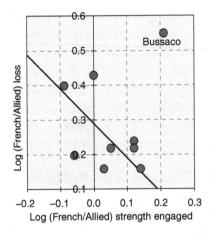

Figure 5 Variation of the ratio of French/Allied losses with the ratio of French/
Allied strengths engaged

and 8,600. Taking an intermediate number of 7,800 gives a French/Allied loss ratio of 7,800/5,800 = 1.34. This ratio was distorted by a surprise attack by French cavalry on three British battalions, causing about 1,000 British and 200 French casualties. For this analysis, focussing on the relative firepower of the opposing armies, it is appropriate to use a French/Allied loss ratio of 7,600/ 4,800 = 1.58.

Salamanca, 22 July 1812 The French army was marching around the right flank of the Allied army, and was correspondingly strung out in marching columns, when the Allied army suddenly took the offensive. The French army was surprised with its divisions widely dispersed, so that some of them did not come into action until others had been routed. The French/Allied strength ratio of troops present on the battlefield was 49,000/52,000 = 0.94 and the ratio of troops actually engaged was 44,000/33,000 = 1.33 (excluding General Foy's French division away to the east and several Allied units which were only lightly engaged), but these ratios are both misleading. The French divisions of Generals Ferey and Sarrut (together 10,700 men) covered the retreat of the beaten French army but were absent from the main action, which involved a French/Allied strength ratio of 33,800/30,200 = 1.12. However the two westerly French divisions – of Generals Thomieres (4,500) and Macune (5,400) – were defeated and routed before they could be supported by other French units. If only one third of these divisions could have been rallied to fight in the rest of the main action, the French/Allied strength ratio in that action, allowing for some British casualties, would have been 27,400/29,500 = 0.93. So a representative strength ratio of troops engaged in the main action was probably about 1.0. In their later rearguard actions, Ferey and Sarrut were probably outnumbered, but it remains unclear how many Allied units were in action during that phase of the battle. Only about half of the French units reported their losses, but it is estimated that their army lost about 14,000; the Allied loss was 4,762. The French loss was inflated by a successful British cavalry charge which probably inflicted 1,500 French losses at the cost of 100 British casualties. For this analysis, focussing on the firepower of the opposing armies, it is appropriate to use a loss ratio of 12,500/4,662 = 2.68

Vitoria, 21 June 1813 The French army retreating from Spain expected to be attacked from the west and deployed accordingly, but part of the allied army looped north through the mountains so the Allies launched simultaneous attacks from the north and west. There were 75,000 Allied and 57,000 French troops present on the battlefield, plus another 20,000 French and Spanish non-combatants travelling with the French army. Two French cavalry brigades (3,000) and several Allied infantry and cavalry brigades were not actively engaged and suffered only trifling losses, so the French/Allied ratio of strength engaged was 54,000/48,000 = 1.13. The reported losses were 8,008 French and 5,158 Allies, but adding estimated losses for the few French units which did not report gives a French/Allied loss ratio of 8,500/5,158 = 1.65 (see Table 5).

Synopsis Figure 5 shows that the data from the Peninsular War battles followed the trend predicted by Lanchester's Square Law, with the exception of Bussaco where the French attacked against very unfavourable terrain. The other results suggest that the individual effectiveness of Allied troops was about double that of the French.

Data Sources for Appendix 4

Calvert, M. (1978) *A Dictionary of Battles 1715–1815*, London: New English Library.

Chandler, D. (1966) *The Campaigns of Napoleon*, New York: Macmillan Publishing.

Dempsey, G. (2011) *Albuera 1811*, Yorkshire: Pen and Sword.

Esdaile, C. (2002) *The Peninsular War*, London: Penguin Press.

Esposito, V. (1999) *A Military History and Atlas of the Napoleonic Wars*. London: Greenhill Books.

Gates, D. (1986) *The Spanish Ulcer*, London: Guild Publishing.

Hibbert, C (1961) *Corunna*, London: Pan Books.

Oman, C. (1995) *A History of the Peninsular War*, London: Greenhill Books.

Smith, D. (1998) *Napoleonic Wars Data Book*, London: Greenhill Books.

Weller, J. (1962) *Wellington in the Peninsula*, London: Greenhill Books.

Appendix 5
Napoleon's Last Campaign in Germany, 1813

Several of the battles of the 1813 campaigns are unsuitable for this analysis because their outcomes either were affected by fortifications or were determined primarily by cavalry operations rather than by firepower (generally because heavy rain disabled the infantry muskets). Others were unsuitable because the defeated army's losses included high proportions of prisoners/ missing and it was unclear whether these losses were incurred during the battle or afterwards; hence the ratio of losses in these battles is particularly ill-defined. Even in the remaining open-field battles which appear to have been decided by firepower, the historical records do not always reveal how many of the troops present were actively engaged so this analysis had to rely on the ratio of the numbers present.

The huge battle of Leipzig was fought in two phases – on 16 October and on 18–19 October 1813. The first phase was fought as three separate engagements at Mockern, at Wachau and at the fortified bridgehead of Lindenau. The second phase was fought around Leipzig itself and, at the end of this phase, the defeated French army retreated on a long causeway across the two rivers Elster and Luppe and the intervening swamp; its losses were inflated by prisoners taken after the premature destruction of the only bridge across the Elster. This decisive battle has been extensively studied, so it is possible to estimate the numbers and losses in the separate engagements (see the following battle summaries).

Lutzen, 2 May At the beginning of this battle, the Allied corps of Generals Blucher, Berg and Yorck attacked Marshal Ney's isolated French corps. The French had a slight superiority of numbers, with a French/Allied strength ratio of $45,000/42,000 = 1.07$ but were disadvantaged by surprise and by a shortage of cavalry. The strength ratio fluctuated through the day as reinforcements arrived and by the end of the battle the French/Allied ratio of troops engaged was $78,000/70,000 = 1.11$. A French/ Allied strength ratio of 1.1 is probably representative. The French/Allied loss ratio is uncertain (the Allies are believed to have under-reported their losses) but was probably about $20,000/18,000 = 1.11$.

Konigswartha, 19 May General Barclay's Russian corps and General Yorck's Prussian corps attacked an isolated French (actually Italian) division. The Prussians did not arrive until the battle was virtually ended, so the French/

Table 6 Battle data from Naploeon's 1813 campaign in Germany

Battle	French strength	Allied strength	French loss	Allied loss	Log F/A Strength engaged	Log F/A Loss in battle	Log A/F effectiveness
Lutzen	78,000	70,000	20,000	18,000	+0.04	+0.05	+0.09
Konigsw'	8,500	17,000	2,500	1,000	−0.31	+0.40	+0.09
Weissig	13,400	7,600	1,800	2,400	+0.25	−0.12	+0.13
Luckau	20,000	15,800	1,850	800	+0.10	+0.43	
Grossbeeren	20,000	30,000	3,000	1,000	−0.17	+0.48	+0.31
Gohrde	4,250	13,000	1,750	530	−0.48	+0.52	+0.04
Mockern	29,000	33,000	9,000	9,000	0	0	0
Wachau	varied	varied	15,200	28,000	+0.10	−0.28	−0.18
Leipzig	146,000	280,000	18,000	13,000	−0.28	+0.14	−0.14
Average of 8							+0.04

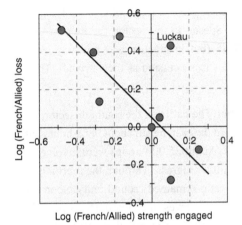

Log (French/Allied) strength engaged

Figure 6 Variation of the ratio of French/Allied losses with ratio of French/
Allied strengths engaged

Allied ratio of troops engaged was about 8,500/17,000 = 0.5 and the corresponding loss ratio was 2,500/1,000 = 2.5.

Weissig (Eichberg), 19 May This battle was a meeting engagement between French and Prussian forces both of which received successive reinforcements. The final French/Allied strength ratio was 13,400/7,600 = 1.75, and the loss ratio was 1,800/2,400 = 0.75.

Luckau, 4 June The French attacked a particularly strong position and were decisively repulsed. The French/Allied strength ratio was 20,000/15,800 = 1.27 and the loss ratio was 1,850/800 = 2.31.

Grossbeeren, 23rd August In this battle, General Reynier's French corps was defeated by General Bulow's Prussian corps; the proportion of these corps effectively engaged is uncertain but the French/Allied strength ratio was probably 0.67. Marshal Oudinot's French corps arrived on the battlefield as darkness fell, too late to influence the outcome. The French/Allied loss ratio was about 3,000/1,000 = 3.

Gohrde, 16 September An isolated French detachment with only a few cavalry was overwhelmed by a much larger Allied force. The French/Allied strength ratio was about 4,250/13,000 = 0.33 and the loss ratio was about 1,750/530 = 3.30.

Mockern, 16 October On the northern sector of the battlefront at Leipzig, Marshal Marmont's French corps and other forces tried to resist attack by

General Yorck's Prussian corps and part of General Langeron's Russian corps of the Allied Army of Silesia. In this sector, the French/Allied strength ratio was 29,000/33,000 = 0.88 (but in practice was probably close to 1.0 since Yorck attacked with brigades in succession as they arrived). The loss ratio was 9,000/9,000 = 1.0.

Wachau, 16 October The battle on the southern sector, from Connewitz in the west to Klein Posna in the east, began about 0800 hours with an allied attack on the French positions. About 35,000 troops were involved on each side, and the Allied attack made little progress. Through the morning reinforcements joined in, but the strength ratio remained around unity. Soon after 1100 h, Emperor Napoleon deployed his reserves (the Guard, IX corps and the Ist, IVth and Vth cavalry corps) and launched a successful counter attack, although some of the troops he has planned to use were diverted to the north and west of Leipzig. The arrival of successive Allied reinforcements through the afternoon after 1400 hours saved the Allied Army of Bohemia from defeat; that Army was battered but not broken. The French/Allied ratio of the number of troops engaged fluctuated through the day from near parity at the beginning and end of the battle to a maximum of 1.5 around noon; a ratio of 1.25 is probably representative. The Allies lost heavily in this sector, yielding a French/Allied loss ratio of 15,000/29,000 = 0.52.

Leipzig, 18–19 October There was little fighting on 17 October, during which the Allies received large reinforcements and Emperor Napoleon withdrew his remaining forces to a perimeter close to Leipzig. He sent General Bertrand's corps westward to clear the road to France and sent two divisions of the Young Guard to hold Lindenau. On the 18th the Allies attacked with 295,000 troops, but the Swedish corps was never actively engaged so the effective French/Allied strength ratio was 146,000/280,000 = 0.52. During the night and the following morning, the French retreated across the causeway to Lindenau until the causeway was destroyed prematurely about 1300 hours, trapping the French rear-guard. During these two days, the French lost about 18,000 men killed and wounded, but about 25,000 more were captured (including the sick in Leipzig hospital) and 5,000 Saxons deserted to the Allies. The French/Allied ratio of killed and wounded in battle over those two days was 18,000/13,000 = 1.38 (see Table 6 and Figure 6).

Synopsis The variations between the loss ratios in the 1813 battles were roughly consistent with Lanchester's Square Law, except for the outlier at Luckau where the Allies occupied a particularly strong defensive position. The individual effectiveness of the Allied soldiers was slightly greater than that of the inexperienced French.

Data Sources for Appendix 5

Calvert, M. (1978) *A Dictionary of Battles 1715–1815*, London: New English Library.

Chandler, D. (1966) *The Campaigns of Napoleon*, New York: Macmillan.

Esposito, V. (1999) *A Military History and Atlas of the Napoleonic Wars*, London: Greenhill Books.

Hofschrorer, P. (1993) *Leipzig 1813*, London: Osprey.

Lawford, J. (1977) *Napoleon's Last Campaigns 1813–15*, London: Book Club Associates.

Nafziger, G. (1992) *Lutzen and Bautzen*, Chicago: The Emperor Press.

Nafziger, G. 1996 *Napoleon at Leipzig* Chicago: The Emperor Press.

Petre, F. (1974) *Napoleon's Last Campaign in Germany*, London: Arms and Armour.

Rothenburg, G. (1997) *The Art of Warfare in the Age of Napoleon*, Kent: Spellmount.

Smith, D, (1998) *Napoleonic Wars Data Book*, London: Greenhill Books.

Smith, D. (2001) *1813 Leipzig*, London: Greenhill Books.

Appendix 6
The Austro-Prussian War, 1866

The Austro-Prussian War of 1866 (also known as the Seven Weeks War) included five corps-level battles along the Bohemian frontier and a conclusive army-level battle farther south near Koniggratz (Sadowa), a fortress on the Elbe. These six battles involved the Prussians fighting against the Austrians and their Saxon allies. Many of the battles were meeting engagements in which the strength ratio of the opposing forces fluctuated as reinforcements arrived and were sent into action, but this analysis has generally assumed that the final ratio is a representative average (except for some special circumstances as noted in the following battle summaries).

The histories of the Seven Weeks War tend to identify the major units which fought in the battles, but do not always specify how many of their sub-units were actually engaged in those battles. For this analysis, it was assumed, whenever there was no better information, that all of the troops present were engaged. The strengths of the opposing forces were calculated from the baselines that, at the start of the war, an Austrian army corps had 31,000 men (the 1st corps had an extra brigade and thus had 36,000) and most Prussian corps had 26,000 but the Guard corps was stronger with 29,000. Later in the war, these totals were reduced by the losses which particular formations had sustained in earlier battles. No allowance was made for the progressive reduction in the strength of the units involved through straggling and sickness. There are some differences in the battle strengths and losses cited in different histories. Craig's data has been used in this analysis unless otherwise stated.

Nachod, 27 June This battle was fought between the Austrian 6th corps and some reserve cavalry and the Prussian V corps of which three battalions were kept in reserve and did not engage. The resulting Austro/Prussian strength ratio was apparently 33,000/23,000 = 1.45. However, the leading Austrian brigade was badly beaten before reinforcements arrived; for this analysis, its impact on the battle was assumed to be reduced to half strength giving a more-representative strength ratio of 29,500/23,000 = 1.28. The Austro/Prussian loss ratio was 5,719/1,122 = 5.10.

Trautenau, 27 June The Austrian 10th corps fought the Prussian I corps giving a Austro/Prussian strength ratio of 31,000/26,000 = 1.19. The Austro/Prussian loss ratio was 4,787/1,338 = 3.58, or possibly higher.

Table 7 Numbers and losses in the 1866 battles

Battle	Austrian strength	Prussian strength	Austrian loss	Prussian loss	Log A/P Strength	Log A/P Loss	Log P/A effectiveness
Nachod	29,500	23,000	5,719	1,122	0.11	0.71	0.82
Traut.	31,000	26,000	4,787	1,338	0.08	0.55	0.63
Skalitz	31,000	31,000	5,500	1,365	0	0.61	0.61
Soor	26,200	29,000	3,819	713	−0.05	0.73	0.68
Gitschin	39,000	26,000	5,511	1,553	0.18	0.55	0.73
Konigg.	221,000	198,000	36,500	9,172	0.05	0.60	0.65
Average of 6							0.69

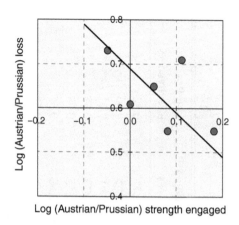

Figure 7 Variation of the ratio of Austrian/Prussian losses ratio with the ratio of Austro-Prussian strengths engaged

Skalitz, 28 June The Austrian 8th corps fought the Prussian V corps which had already incurred casualties at Nachod, but had been reinforced by a brigade of the VI corps. The Austro/Prussian strength ratio was 31,000/31,000 = 1.00. The Austro/Prussian loss ratio was 5,500/1,365 = 4.02.

Soor, 28 June The Prussian Guard corps fought the Austrian 10th corps which was already depleted and demoralised by its losses at Trautenau. The Austro/Prussian strength ratio was 26,200/29,000 = 0.90 and the loss ratio was 3,819/713 = 5.36.

Gitschin, 29 June The Prussian 3rd and 5th divisions (together about equivalent to a Prussian corps) fought an Austro-Saxon force of seven brigades (five Austrian and two Saxon) of which two brigades were kept in reserve and used only to cover the retreat. For this analysis, the impact of those two brigades was assumed to be reduced to half strength, giving a Austro/Prussian strength ratio of 39,000/26,000 = 1.5 and the loss ratio was 5,511/1,553 = 3.55.

Koniggratz, 3 July The Austrian Army of the North (then some 221,000 strong including Saxon allies) deployed along the small river Bistritz with artillery emplaced on the heights behind; its right and left flanks were refused (i.e. bent rearward) towards the river Elbe which flowed behind the Austrian army. It was attacked on 3 July by two Prussian armies – the First Army (94,000) and the Elbe Army (60,000) – but through the morning they made little progress. The fighting was fiercest on the Prussian left where up to nineteen battalions of the Prussian IV corps advanced into a wood (the Swiepwald) and were engaged there by up to fifty Austrian battalions from the 4th and 2nd corps. In this close-quarters fighting, the Austrians were at a severe tactical disadvantage against the rapid fire of the Prussians' breech-loading rifles, and suffered many casualties. In the afternoon, the Prussian Second Army (109,000) joined the battle and drove into the (weakened and demoralised) right flank of the Austrian army, forcing it to make a disorderly retreat towards the Elbe bridges.

Not all of the Prussian units in those three armies were engaged in active operations. Only the two leading divisions (the 14th and 15th) of the Elbe Army came into action against the Austrian left flank. Of the Prussian Second Army on the other flank, only the Guard corps, the VI corps and a few battalions of other corps were heavily engaged. It follows that the Austro/Prussian ratio of troops engaged was 221,000/198,000 = 1.12. The Prussian armies lost 9,172 men. The total losses of the Austrian and Saxon army were 44,313, but this number includes 7,836 missing who were mostly soldiers drowned in the river Elbe after the battle and stragglers who had not rejoined their units when musters were compiled. It follows that the Austro/Prussian ratio of battle losses was 36,500/9,172 = 3.98 (see Table 7 and Figure 7).

Synopsis Since there were only six battles between Austrians and Prussians, and since the strength ratios on these battles were not very different, the results presented below do not provide conclusive support for Lanchester's Square Law. They are however reasonably consistent with that Law. The data from these six battles suggest that the individual effectiveness of a Prussian soldier was about five times greater than that of an Austrian. This factor reflects the superiority of the Prussian breech-loading rifle as well as the faulty Austrian tactical doctrine and the ineptitude of some aristocratic Austrian commanders.

Data Sources for Appendix 6

Anderson, J. (1912) *The Austro-Prussian War in Bohemia 1866*, London: Hugh Rees.

Bonnal, H. (1913) *Sadowa – a Study*, London: Hugh Rees.

Craig, G. (1964) *The Battle of Koniggratz*, New York: Lippincott Co.

Hozier, H. (1907) *The Seven Weeks War*, London: Macmillan and Co.

Wagner, A. (1899) *The Campaign of Koniggratz*, Kansas City: Hudson Kimberley Publishing.

Table 8 Published numbers and losses in some 1870 battles

Battle	French strength	German strength	French loss	German loss	Log F/G Strength	Log F/G Loss	Log G/F Effect.
Wissembourg	7,500	92,000	2,300	1,500	−1.09	+0.18	−0.91
Vionville	123,000	63,000	16,900	15,800	+0.29	+0.03	+0.32
Gravelotte	120,000	200,000	12,300	20,200	−0.22	−0.21	−0.43

Appendix 7

The Franco-Prussian War, 1870

The analysis presented in this Appendix covers the first phase of the Franco-Prussian war, and the results of the battles between the German armies (including Bavarians and other allied contingents who were perhaps less enthusiastic and well-disciplined than the Prussians) and the French Imperial armies in August and September 1870. In the second phase of the war, after the main Imperial armies had surrendered at Sedan and Metz, the Germans fought against improvised French Republican armies with very variable levels of morale, leadership, training and equipment. All of these factors obscured the effect of the relative numbers in the opposing armies, so this second phase of the war is entirely unsuitable for analysis.

There were insufficient battles in the first phase of this war to generate an adequate database, but it is nevertheless appropriate to review them rigorously, because the published numbers and losses in some battles yielded very diverse values of German/French effectiveness (see Table 8). If these effectiveness values were valid, they would weaken the credibility of Lanchester's combat models.

In this war, retreating soldiers with rifles were still able to resist pursuing cavalry, so it is reasonable to assume that most of the defeated French soldiers 'missing' in a battle were captured as a direct result of the battle rather than in the later retreat.

Wissembourg, 4 August In this battle, General Douay's French division should have had 9,000 men at full strength but, because of the chaotic nature of the French mobilisation, it probably had around 7,000 that day (estimates vary from 6,000 to 8,600). It was able to take some advantage of the buildings and seventeenth-century fortifications of Wissembourg. It was heavily outnumbered by the three German corps (V, XI and II Bavarian, totalling 92,000 men with 44 artillery batteries) present on the battlefield but it is unlikely that all of these German troops could have been effectively engaged. Since only eleven German artillery batteries out of forty-four went into action that day, it is reasonable to assume that about a quarter of the German troops present were actually engaged. Hence the French/German ratio of troops engaged was probably about $7,000/23,000 = 0.30$. Most histories agree that the French/German loss ratio was $2,300/1,550 = 1.48$.

Worth, 6th August 1870 The French army at Worth consisted of Marshal MacMahon's 1st corps, a division from the 7th corps, and a division of reserve cavalry. These units had a nominal strength of 51,000 men, but the army was understrength because of mobilisation problems and because of losses at Wissembourg. For this analysis, its strength is estimated to have been 45,000 men. The German army consisted of four army corps (the V and XI Prussian, and the I and II Bavarian), with a total strength of 125,000. However, only a part of the I Bavarian corps came into action (late in the battle) so the German strength engaged was probably about 91,000 men. Hence the representative French/German ratio of troops engaged was estimated to be 45,000/91,000 = 0.49, which is consistent with most histories. Various accounts of the battle quote French/German loss ratios of between 1.5 and 2.0, with the most authoritative estimate being 18,200/10,500 = 1.73. However the loss ratio in this battle was distorted by gallant but futile charges by French cavalry which suffered severe losses but inflicted no significant losses on the Germans. Excluding the losses in these sacrificial charges, the French/German losses due to firepower was (18,200 − 2,400)/10,500 = 1.50.

Spichern, 6 August 1870 At the start of this battle, the leading troops of the German VII corps were outnumbered by the French 2nd corps in a good (and perhaps partially entrenched) defensive position, but successive reinforcements gave the Germans superiority of numbers by the end of the battle. The French probably had about 26,000 men, whereas the German VII corps and a brigade of the III corps had together about 36,000, giving a French/German strength ratio of 26,000/36,000 = 0.72 at the end of the battle. For this analysis, it seems reasonable to adopt a representative value of 0.9 for the battle as a whole. Most histories agree that the French/German loss ratio was 0.8.

Borny, 15 August 1870 This unintended and inconclusive battle is largely ignored in histories of the war. It appears to have involved the German I and VII corps plus part of the IX corps, with a strength of about 71,000 men, against the French 3rd and 4th corps with a nominal strength of 72,000 men. Assuming that the French units were understrength, it is reasonable to estimate the French/German strength ratio at 0.9. The French/German loss ratio is also uncertain, but was probably about 0.71.

Vionville, 16 August 1870 This battle (also known as Rezonville/Mars la Tour) was an unexpected meeting engagement where the troops engaged on both sides increased progressively through the day. The traditional histories suggest that two gallant German corps (the III and later the X) fought the entire French Army of the Rhine which had a numerical advantage of 4:1 in the morning and 2:1 in the late afternoon. In reality, some units in the Army of the Rhine (the infantry divisions of Generals Metman and Lorencez) did not arrive on the battlefield until the fighting was over, and other divisions were present but were hardly engaged (General Sorval's infantry and General Clerambault's cavalry). Although the Army of the Rhine, after its losses at Spichern and Borny, had some 123,000 men nominally available, only 97,000 actually fought.

In the morning action, the German III corps fought the French understrength 2nd corps, which was the most westerly of the French units. The French 6th corps was nearby but chose to deploy to the right and a mile to the rear of the 2nd, and thus took virtually no part in this engagement. In this phase, the French/German strength ratio of troops engaged was about 0.75 and most of the 2nd corps was forced to retreat. It was then redeployed in reserve and was replaced in the firing line by a division of the French Imperial Guard.

In the early afternoon, a tentative advance by the French 6th corps was checked by a heroic charge by part of a German cavalry brigade, after which the disordered 6th corps played only a minor role in the battle. Later, the French 3rd and 4th corps gradually extended the French line of battle to the west. These two French corps vastly outnumbered the German forces (part of 37th brigade) on this part of the battlefield, but their gradual advance was checked by German counterattacks and by the arrival of the German X corps. These two French corps both lacked one or more of their infantry divisions, absent or detached, which may have eroded the confidence of their commanders. Near the end of the day, the opposing cavalry forces both sought to outflank the western end of the enemy line of battle, resulting in a spectacular but inconclusive action near Mars la Tour.

At the eastern end of the battlefield, the French amassed nearly half of their forces between Rezonville and Gravelotte, to preclude a possible German offensive northward along the river Meuse which would cut off the French army from its supply base at Metz. These French units took virtually no part in the battle until the late evening, when some of them repelled attacks by small advance guards of the German VIII and IX corps.

Since various units of both opposing armies came into action at different times, and since the intensity of the fighting varied through the day, it is difficult to derive a representative French/German ratio of the number of troops engaged. For this analysis a time-averaged number of troops engaged was calculated for both armies, and this (inevitably approximate) procedure yielded a ratio of 1.00. This value is a speculative estimate which might be improved by a more-detailed analysis, but it may be used in this analysis for lack of anything better. There is a general consensus that the French/German loss ratio was $16,900/15,800 = 1.07$.

It should be noted that the current French tactical doctrine was defensive, playing to the strengths of the Chassepot rifle and the Mitrailleuse machine gun. Thus when a French force encountered an enemy, the French commander deployed in a good position and waited to be attacked (this approach may

Table 9 Strength engaged and losses in 1870 battles

Battle	French strength	German strength	French loss	German loss	Log F/G Strength engaged	Log F/G Loss in battle	Log G/F Effect.
Wissembourg	7,000	23,000	2,300	1,500	-0.52	+0.17	
Worth	45,000	91,000	15,800	10,500	-0.31	+0.18	-0.13
Spichern	26,000	36,000	4,000	5,000	-0.05	-0.10	-0.15
Borny	72,000	71,000	3,500	5,000	-0.05	-0.15	-0.20
Vionville	97,000	63,000	16,900	15,800	0	+0.03	+0.03
Gravelotte	100,000	150,000	12,300	20,200	-0.18	-0.21	
Sedan	124,000	160,000	38,000	9,000	-0.11	+0.62	
Average of 4							-0.11

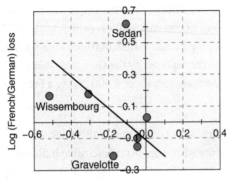

Figure 8 Variation of the ratio of French/German losses with the ratio of Franco/German strengths engaged

have been reinforced by reports of the huge Austrian losses in 1866 when they had rashly attacked Prussian infantry with breech-loading rifles). The defensive French doctrine meant that at Vionville the French commanders were reluctant to attack and thus they failed to exploit their superior numbers present on the battlefield. Hence the time-averaged ratio of numbers engaged is very much smaller than the ratio of numbers present.

Gravelotte, 18 August 1870 In this set-piece battle, it is known that some of the defending French corps (2nd and 3rd) reduced their losses by constructing field fortifications. The French/German ratio of troops on the battlefield was 120,000/200,000 = 0.6; however 20,000 men of the French Imperial Guard were kept in reserve, as were two (the III and X) of the eight German corps present, so the French/ German ratio of troops engaged was probably about 100,000/150,000 = 0.67. The French/German loss ratio was 12,300/20,200 = 0.61.

Sedan, 1 September 1870 Because political imperatives overruled military strategy, the French Army of Chalons marched into a position around the obsolete fortress of Sedan, which was outstandingly unfavourable (and was described by General Ducrot as a chamber pot). In that position, it was progressively surrounded by twice as many German troops, which attacked from all directions. Some French units resisted very gallantly, but others became increasingly demoralised by a concentric hail of German artillery fire (on top of the hunger, fatigue and confusion which they had endured through the preceding days) and ceased to offer any effective resistance even before the Emperor Napoleon III surrendered himself and his army. Several German units (the IV, VI and half of the II Bavarian} remained in reserve or on the other side of the river Meuse, so the infantry in these corps was not closely engaged. The French/German ratio of troops engaged was probably about 124,000/160,000 = 0.78. During the battle the French lost 38,000 men killed, wounded and captured (and another 86,000 were captured by the Germans or interned in Belgium after the surrender). The Germans lost about 9,000 giving a French/German loss ratio of 4.2.

Synopsis Seven battles were considered in this analysis. At Wissembourg, the French could take some advantage from defensible buildings; at Gravelotte, the French losses were reduced because at least half of their army was entrenched; and at Sedan, the French losses were atypically inflated because their army was demoralised by exhaustion, scant supplies and earlier defeats, and because it had deployed in a very unfavourable position dominated by encircling German artillery. The strength and loss ratios of these seven battles are presented in Table 9 and Figure 8.

The data from the four battles (Worth to Vionville) which were not affected by the special circumstances noted previously are roughly consistent with Lanchester's Square Law, but they are too few (and the estimated strength ratios are too uncertain) to provide conclusive support. The average German/French effectiveness for these four battles suggests that the individual effectiveness of the French Imperial troops engaged exceeded that of the Germans (perhaps by 25 per cent) because of the extra range of their Chassepot rifles. However the French armies were still defeated because the Germans mobilised twice as many troops and manoeuvred them more effectively. The results from Wissenbourg and Gravelotte show that the German/French effectiveness ratios in these battles was significantly lower, being affected by field fortifications.

Data Sources for Appendix 7

Ascoli, D. (1982) *A Day of Battle*, London: Harrap.
Barry, Q. (2007) *The Franco-Prussian War 1879–71*, Warwick, UK: Helion and Co.
Elliot-Wright, P. (1993) *Gravelotte-St.Privat 1870*, London: Osprey.
Guedella, P. (1943) *The Two Marshals*, London: Hodder and Stoughton.
Howard M. (1961) *The Franco-Prussian War*, London: Rupert Hart-Davis.
Howes P (1998) *The Catalytic Wars*, London: Minerva Press.
Pratt S. (1914) *Saarbruck to Paris*, London: George Allen and Co.
Showalter D. (2004) *The Wars of German Unification*, London: Hodder Arnold.
Wawro G. (2003) *The Franco-Prussian War*, Cambridge: Cambridge University Press.

References

Augustine, N. (1983) *Augustine's Laws*, New York: American Institute of Aeronautics and Astronautics.

Bennett, G. (1967) *Coronel and the Falkland Islands*, London: Pan Books.

Busse, J. (1971) *An Attempt to Verify Lanchester's Equations*, Proceedings of the Third Israel Conference on Operational Research.

Chandler, D. (2002) *The Military Maxims of Napoleon; Maxim 29*, London: Greenhill Books.

Davis, W. 1983 *The Civil War*, Virginia: Time-Life Books.

Dupuy, T. (1985) *Numbers, Prediction and War*, Virginia: Hero Books.

Eccles, N. (1999) Validation and Tactical Decision Making in Generalised Lanchester Combat Models, Cranfield University thesis, unpublished.

Engel, J. (1954) A Verification of Lanchester's Law, Operations Research, Volume 2, pp. 163–171.

Epstein, J. (1985) *The Calculus of Conventional War*, Washington, DC: Brookings Institution.

Fain, J. (1977) The Lanchester Equations and Historical Warfare, *History, Numbers and War* Volume 1, pp. 34–52.

Foote, S. (1963) *The Civil War: a Narrative*, New York: Random House.

Ford, R. (1998) *The Tiger Tank*, Kent: Spellmount,

Fricker, D. (1998) Attrition Models of the Ardennes Campaign, *Naval Research Logistics* Volume 45, pp. 1–22.

Fuller, J. (1958) *The Generalship of Ulysses S. Grant*, New York: Plenum Publishing.

Gilbert, M. (1994) *First World War*, London: Weidenfeld and Nicholson.

Halpern, P. G. (1994) *A Naval History of World War I*, London: University College London Press.

Hayman, P. (1980) *References on the Lanchester Theory of Combat to 1980*, England: RMCS.

James, L. (1998) *Raj: the Making and Unmaking of British India*, London: The Softback Preview.

Kaldor, M. (1982) *The Baroque Arsenal*, London: Andre Deutsch.

Kennedy, F. (1990) *The Civil War Battlefield Guide*, Boston: Houghton Mufflin.

Kirkpatrick, D. (1985) Do Lanchester's Equations Adequately Model Real Battles? *RUSI Journal* June pp. 25–27.

Kishi, T. (1961) *The Lanchester Theory of Combat*, unpublished.

Lanchester, F. (1916) *Aircraft in Warfare; Dawn of the Fourth Arm*, London: Constable and Co.

Livermore, T. (1901) *Numbers and Losses in the Civil War in America*, Ohio, Riverside Press.

McPherson, J. (1982) *Ordeal by Fire: The Civil War and Reconstruction*, New York: Knopf.

McPherson, J. (1988) *Battle Cry of Freedom*, Oxford University Press.

McWhiney, G. (1982) *Attack and Die*, University of Alabama Press.

Macksey K. (1988) *Tank versus Tank*, London, Bantam Press.

Macksey K. (2006) *Why the Germans Lose at War*, London, Greenhill Books.

Mead, G. (2008) *The Good Soldier – the Biography of Douglas Haig*, London: Atlantic Books.

Overy, R. (2001) *The Battle of Britain*, New York: Norton and Co.

Sears, S. (1992) *To the Gates of Richmond*, New York: Ticknor and Fields.

Underwood, R. ed., (1887) *Battles and Leaders of the Civil War*, New Jersey: Castle.

Voltaire, F. (1770) *Lettre a M. le Riche, 6th February*

Weiss, H. (1957) Lanchester-type Models of Warfare, Proceedings of International Conference on Operational Research pp. 82–99, Oxford September.

Weiss, H. (1966) Combat Models and Historical Data; the US Civil War, *Operations Research* Volume 14, pp. 759–790

Willard, D. (1962) *Lanchester as a Force in History*, unpublished.

Wood, D., and Dempster D. (1961) *The Narrow Margin*, London:Hutchinson.

About the Author

David Kirkpatrick is Emeritus Professor of Defence Analysis at University College London.

Cambridge Elements ≡

Defence Economics

Keith Hartley
University of York

Keith Hartley was Professor of Economics and Director of the Centre for Defence Economics at the University of York, where he is now Emeritus Professor of Economics. He is the author of over 500 publications comprising journal articles, books and reports. His most recent books include *The Economics of Arms* (Agenda Publishing, 2017) and with Jean Belin (Eds.) *The Economics of the Global Defence Industry* (Taylor and Francis, 2020). Hartley was founding Editor of the journal *Defence and Peace Economics*; a NATO Research Fellow; a QinetiQ Visiting Fellow; consultant to the UN, EC, EDA, UK MoD, HM Treasury, Trade and Industry, Business, Innovation and Skills and International Development and previously Special Adviser to the House of Commons Defence Committee.

About the Series

Defence Economics is a relatively new field within the discipline of economics. It studies all aspects of the economics of war and peace. It embraces a wide range of topics in both macroeconomics and microeconomics. Cambridge Elements in Defence Economics aims to publish original and authoritative papers in the field. These will include expert surveys of the foundations of the discipline, its historical development and contributions developing new and novel topics. They will be valuable contributions to both research and teaching in universities and colleges, and will also appeal to other specialist groups comprising politicians, military and industrial personnel as well as informed general readers.

Cambridge Elements $^{\equiv}$

Defence Economics

CPSIA information can be obtained
at www.ICGtesting.com
Printed in the USA
LVHW011949190821
695611LV00005B/666

9 781108 977876